The Lost World of the
Great Spas

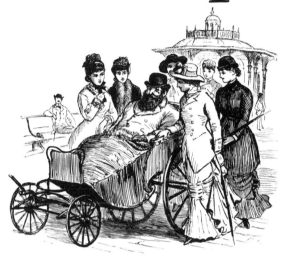

Endpapers A nineteenth-century
engraving of Karlsbad in
Czechoslovakia, showing the central
architectural features of the town and
the local springs.

above An invalid in a bath chair on
Brighton pier.

overleaf right An early nineteenth-
century water-colour of Bath by
Nattes showing the King's Bath.

The Lost World of the
Great Spas

Joseph Wechsberg

with additional material by
Ruth Brandon

1817

Harper & Row, Publishers
New York, Hagerstown, San Francisco, London

THE LOST WORLD OF THE GREAT SPAS

FIRST U.S. EDITION

ISBN: 0–06–014584–6

LIBRARY OF CONGRESS CATALOG CARD NUMBER: LC 79–1691

Contents

Foreword

A 'spa' is defined by Webster as 'a mineral spring', and is now generally meant to be a place with cold or hot springs that are believed to have healing powers. Historically, the name comes from the small town of Spa in the Belgian Ardennes, not far from Liège, where for centuries famous people went 'to take the waters', sipping or bathing. The water at Spa would cure heart diseases, rheumatism and all kinds of respiratory inflammations. Marguerite de Valois, Queen Christina of Sweden, Tsar Peter the Great and Victor Hugo were all visitors there, and Kaiser Wilhelm II even selected the place for his abdication.

Spa already had all the necessary attributes: a beautiful location, a large park, clean air, a gambling casino and a somewhat glistening past. No spa is better than its reputation, which often rests on the visitors rather than the springs. In the eighteenth and nineteenth centuries, each spa worth its weight in mineral salts had its list of crowned heads and celebrities who came there to get well and have fun.

The pleasant institution outlived the feudal centuries and is now enthusiastically accepted by social-medicine patients and private health seekers. In certain countries of Europe a mystical belief exists that there is a spa for practically every affliction of body and mind. Some swear by one spa, others go from one to the next in search of salvation. The spa doctor is as powerful a person in Europe as the analyst in America. No patient would dare take a step without his consent. At one time the spa doctor was considered by members of his profession a not very able practitioner who was merely content to have an easy job in pleasant surroundings. Today spa doctors are often eminent specialists who take their patients and their treatments seriously. A spa is no longer a place for only rich old people with a hypochondriac state of mind, but also a place for the poor and the young already afflicted by the ills of our ruthless civilization.

During the nineteenth century some marriage contracts in Germany contained a clause which gave the wife the right to one spa visit a year, alone. In turn the husband would also go to a spa, alone. A wise precaution. The wife or the husband would take the waters, lead a different life – different from the deadly routine at home – and return after three or four weeks, refreshed in body, heart and mind. A spa was like an ocean liner. You enjoyed the inner freedom that comes from knowing that you will probably never meet those aboard again.

Each spa had its *chronique scandaleuse* and its glamorous affairs, as though the healing waters had a stimulating effect. Many spas claim to give the patient a second or third youth, and is there anybody who does not want to be young again? In Germany, the spa paradise, there are even resorts that offer nothing but clean air. Serious doctors would smile at a place calling itself a *Luftkurort*, clean-air-resort, but now they no longer smile.

They know that millions of people are slowly poisoned in the polluted cities. People who go to these health resorts immediately feel better. Spa managements which once considered gambling casinos and racetracks a must have added modern health centres, sports, and treatments for stress and other modern diseases. People are told to relax, to forget the surroundings they came from, to change their pace of life for a while. Exactly what the sociologists and doctors prescribe.

Once upon a time the socially ambitious would go to a spa to see and be seen. The rich wanted to be near the aristocrats and the aristocrats enjoyed the presence of kings. Today the annual visit to a spa is still an important status symbol. Though the fame of the spa rests on its past, it has a healthy present and a secure future.

The main square of the small town, Spa, in the Belgian Ardennes, from which comes the word spa.

Bath

The first-century Roman Baths still
harbour the natural hot springs which
flow underneath Bath. The Abbey,
built in the time of Henry VII, towers
behind.

Bath is Britain's contribution to balneology. It is a spa fitting Webster's definition, 'a mineral spring'. Tests show that the waters of Bath, known of long before the Romans came there, contain some thirty minerals and elements, among them calcium, magnesium, lead, potassium, iron and strontium. The water is slightly radioactive and tastes of sulphur and bismuth. A quarter of a million gallons of water at a constant temperature of 120 degrees Fahrenheit gush out of the earth every twenty-four hours in Bath.

Anywhere but in Britain, the hot springs of Bath would have been expanded into a healthy commercial enterprise. But in Bath the official guide book says, 'Whether (the water) really can do anything for rheumatism, gout, diseases of the nervous system, skin conditions, dyspepsia and anaemia, as innumerable scholarly treatises have claimed, is doubtful.' By the same standard, the healing powers of at least half the spas mentioned in this book would also be 'doubtful'.

The small city of Bath, set between the Cotswolds and the rolling green hills of Somerset, has many attractions. Bath is a city of the Roman past, of kings and cathedrals, of Georgian architecture, of beautiful houses, of Richard Nash, Ralph Allen and John Wood. Bath became fashionable, and attracted royalty and the rich. A trust has now been formed to restore the old treatment centre at the Old Royal Bath, and appeals have been launched to finance the restoration of the former pools. 'Advanced techniques of physiotherapy and hydrotherapy will be used and the Bath Spa Trust hopes to promote medical research as well as serving those who wished to benefit from the springs.'

Sooner or later people in Britain are bound to realize that they do not have to visit the fashionable spas on the Continent, because they have hot springs of their own. In the first century AD the Romans, who were no fools where hot springs were concerned, built what later became the King's Bath. Underneath it is the invisible torrent that brings in the hot waters. The hot springs are piped to the city's swimming pools, and on certain occasions it is possible to bathe in the Roman Baths themselves. And the water can be drunk in the Pump Room and at the fountain in Stall Street.

It was the Pump Room, first built in 1706, when people knew nothing about the Romans and their occupation, which became the 'focal point of the city's social life' for over two hundred and fifty years. It is used today for concerts and other social occasions, and people go there for morning coffee and afternoon tea. Some step to the pump and 'take the waters' but they do not actually believe in it. There are too many other attractions in Bath.

The legend of the founding of Bath is well known. Prince Bladud, the favourite son of Hudibras, contracted leprosy, was banished from his father's court and earned his living as a swineherd. The pigs also suffered from some skin disease. They found the muddy pools in the valley, went into the warm waters and – were cured. Bladud naturally also entered the water and was healed. He returned to his father's court, turned the swamp into a spa and gave it his name, Bladud, later Bad-Lud, Bath Waters. Alas, in the end he fell to his death like Icarus, when the sun melted the wings of a flying machine he had invented. A likely story.

It is no legend, though, that the Romans, great admirers of hot springs, turned the small town into a fashionable resort which was dedicated to the goddess Sul Minerva and became known as Aquae Sulis. During four centuries, the hot springs of Aquae Sulis were famous all over the Roman Empire; the same hot springs that still gush out of the earth today.

Then the Romans and the glory disappeared. 'The country was laid waste by internal warfare and foreign invasion', the history books report. In AD 410 the Emperor Honorius received a plea for help from Britain, which had fallen prey to foreign invaders – the Picts, Saxons, Scots, Irish. But the Romans were unable and unwilling to save Britain and their former health resort.

However, history continued to be made in Bath: on Whit Sunday, AD 973, King Edgar was crowned there in a Saxon abbey 'of wonderful workmanship'. And William Rufus appointed his physician, John de Villula, Bishop of Bath. His job was to replace the little abbey with a great cathedral, and to restore the baths so that 'sick persons from all England resorted thither to bathe in these healing waters and the strong also, to see those wonderful waters and bathe in them'. The baths were restored. Pilgrims came there to seek comfort and healing in the monastic hospitals. St John's, founded by Bishop Reginald in 1180, is today one of the charitable

A panoramic view of Bath and the hills of the Cotswolds drawn in the late eighteenth century, showing the sweeping Georgian terraces and dominating structure of the Abbey.

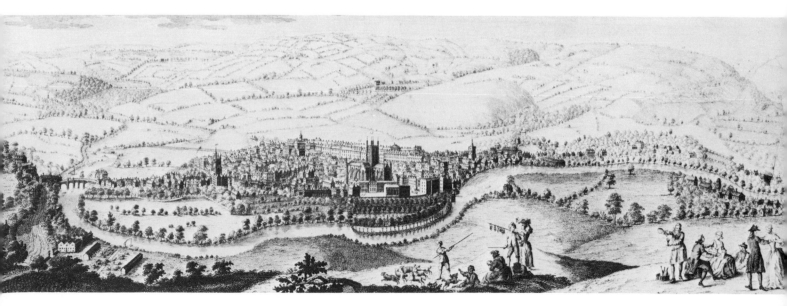

The West front of the Abbey. The angels mounting the ladders either side of the great window are an interesting feature. The Abbey became known as the 'Lantern of the West' because of the huge expanse of windows lighting the nave.

institutions in Bath. People living at the Priory were said to reach 'an astonishing age', which was attributed to the mild climate of the valley and to the power of the healing waters.

But the fame of Bath at that time rested not in its springs but in its reputation as a 'city of weavers', and it became an important manufacturing town. The English were always more interested in broad looms than hot springs. Bath became prosperous, but prosperity brought corruption and decay to city and to church. The once famous baths became 'stinking cisterns'. Henry VI spoke of bathing at Bath as 'beastly'. Henry VII, however, liked to go there, but he was perhaps less attracted by the Cross Bath than by the gaming tables. At that time Bishop Oliver King had the present abbey built and he made Bath Abbey, 'the lantern of the West', one of the wonders of England. It is a graceful, great structure and has a wealth of tablets and memorials.

Queen Elizabeth I came to Bath in 1574 and ordered a national fund to be set up to restore the Abbey and St John's Hospital. She criticized the foul conditions of the streets. However, her Treasury Minister, Lord Burleigh, assured her that 'unsavoury town' could become 'a most sweet town'. The sewers were covered, the streets cleaned, the Abbey restored and the baths made cleaner. Physicians and apothecaries came to the spa, often outnumbering their patients, and studied the waters. Sick people came there at the recommendation of distinguished persons, 'who received gifts and rewards from the mayor'. Royal visits increased throughout the sixteenth and seventeenth centuries.

The five baths were open to the sky and 'exceedingly dirty'. They were even described as 'lewd and immoral'. But James I's wife, Queen Anne, still came in 1613 and 1625 to find a cure for dropsy. The crowds soon followed.

'Methinks', wrote Samuel Pepys, the diarist, in 1668, 'it cannot be clean to get so many bodies together in the same water.' Ladies bathed in garments made of fine yellow canvas with great sleeves like a parson's gown, according to Celia Fiennes' diary, and 'the gentlemen have waistcoats and drawers of the same material'. Musicians played from a gallery in the Cross Bath. Visitors promenaded around the King's Bath to watch the bathers. A lieutenant from Norwich wrote:

. . . English and French, men and women, boyes and girls, one with another, peep up in their caps and appear so nakedly and fearfully in their naked uncouth postures. . . it would a little astonish and put one in mind of the Resurrection.

Pepys admitted that Bath had 'many good streets and very fair stone houses', but John Evelyn found it small and colourless. There was no large

The King's and Queen's
Baths from a drawing by
Thomas Johnson in 1575. The
baths were open, as a cure, to
any of the general public who
were suffering from diseases,
and many bathed naked. This
was heartily disapproved of
by the city authorities and
Samuel Pepys considered it
unhygienic, but it continued
for many years.

hall for public entertainment. The inns were overcrowded, and visitors were charged exorbitant prices for poor accommodation.

But there were fashionable people who held private parties in the taverns where they stayed. Dancing took place on the bowling green east of the Abbey. The Town Common served as a promenade for walking and horse riding. Travelling players entertained their elegant audiences in the Bear Inn Yard, now Union Street. In the Sawclose there were exhibitions of cock-fighting.

Daniel Defoe came to Bath in the early years of the eighteenth century and wrote, 'We may say now it is the resort of the sound as well as of the sick and a place that helps the indolent and the gay to commit that worst of murders – to kill time.' In 1705 a young man from London came to 'kill time' in the spa that Queen Anne had made known. His name was Richard Nash and he was thirty-one. He was born in Carmarthen, had been sent down from Oxford after a scandal, and had lived off his wits, mostly by gambling. He eventually found his kingdom in Bath. There he became the arbiter of taste and society's benevolent despot. He was appointed Master of Ceremonies by the Corporation, but he did more than simply organize parties. (He still liked gambling and won a thousand pounds in his first season. People were delighted because he had arrived at the spa poor.) He became a first-rate public relations expert. He cracked down on beggars and hooligans, and also on dukes and countesses who wore improper dress or entered the ballroom in riding boots. He made sure that the streets were safe to walk in at night. He opened a hospital for the cure of rheumatic diseases, and in 1706 opened the first Pump Room where people could meet 'in civilized company'. It was he who turned Bath into a centre of fashion.

Soon everybody who was anybody came to Bath. People would dance at night in Harrison's Assembly Rooms on the Lower Walks, or they would visit Dame Lindsay's gambling house across the road. 'Beau' Nash, according to the biography which Oliver Goldsmith later wrote of him, was a kindly man, never snobbish or pompous, and gave a great deal of money to charity. He saw to it that prominent visitors were welcomed to the city by the ringing of the Abbey bells. People would meet in the morning at the Pump Room and would drink their three glasses of water while the music played. This was the 'School for Scandal' which inspired Sheridan. Dames and damsels, it was said, would saunter towards the Parade, to take the air and meet people. Alexander Pope, who thought the promenade was the finest in England, walked there with Thomas Parnell and John Gay. Nash died at the age of eighty-eight; he left gambling debts and law-suits but he had a magnificent funeral and his statue and portrait are now in the Pump Room.

opposite A view of Spa, the original spa town, in the Belgian Ardennes.

overleaf left The Roman baths, built in the first century AD, when the Romans first discovered the hot springs in Bath

overleaf right – top A cartoon by Rowlandson from the series, 'Comforts of Bath'; here patients queue up for the waters at the Pump Room.

overleaf right – bottom An early water-colour of Queen Square, Bath, designed by John Wood in 1735.

COMFORTS of BATH.

Pl 3

right 'Beau' Nash after a painting by William Hoare. Nash, appointed master of ceremonies in the early eighteenth century, became not only the arbiter of taste but a great social reformer and advocate of civilized behaviour.

far right Ralph Allen by Thomas Hudson, 1754. One of the major architects of Georgian Bath, he was responsible for Prior Park and many of the streets and houses in Bath.

opposite A corner of the Royal Crescent in Bath, designed by John Wood's son in the 1770s. One hundred and fourteen ionic columns support the continuous cornice.

The second man to make Bath famous was Ralph Allen, who came there in 1710 and was made postmaster. The postal service was in chaos, and Allen promised to make it efficient in return for a seven-year concession. He would pay the government two thousand pounds. Allen made a fortune and bought the stone quarries at Combe Down, the southern hill of Bath. Noted architects in London said that the pale limestone there was useless, but Allen thought he knew better. He agreed with a young architect from Yorkshire, John Wood, who admired the great sixteenth-century Italian humanist and architect, Andrea Palladio. John Wood became Allen's technical adviser. He wanted to make Bath a great neo-classical city in the style of Palladio; Allen provided the stone. They built a tramway to carry the stone from Combe Down to Widcombe and the river. It went past Allen's mansion of Prior Park, a beautiful example of Palladian architecture, which is now a boys' school. It is a fine building with a beautiful view, and there is a Palladian bridge in the grounds.

The unlikely triumvirate of Nash, Allen and Wood created a new image for Bath. Nash managed to attract the high and the mighty in society. Allen and Wood created the fine houses, the walks and streets. All three worked at the creation of the Royal Mineral Water Hospital, which is now the Royal National Hospital for rheumatic diseases. John Wood slowly and methodically turned mediaeval Bath into a Georgian town. He completed his first group of buildings in Queen Square in 1735. On the north side he produced the fine Palladian style which is now much admired. His vision for a Grand Parade on the south side was frustrated by the difficulty of obtaining sites. He built the King's Circus, with a curved façade in three

tiers after all three Doric, Ionic and Corinthian manners. John Wood never saw his work completed. He died at his house, 9 Queen Square, in May, 1754, three months after the Circus was begun. His son, John Wood the younger, completed his father's designs and created his own. His masterpiece was the Royal Crescent, which has been called 'the finest crescent of Europe'. It is over two hundred yards long, with a hundred and fourteen Ionic columns supporting a continuous cornice. It was built between 1767 and 1775, and later many artists, writers and musicians lived there. Other important architects who added to the unique beauty of Bath were Thomas Jelly, Thomas Baldwin, John Palmer and Robert Adam.

left The interior of the Pump Room in the late nineteenth century. Elegant ladies and gentlemen sipped the waters while promenading, accompanied by the music of the orchestra.

above An illustration from the *Bath Guide*. The Guide was published annually, and included many of Nash's moral verses and tales.

Though Bath has been called 'the Florence of the North', it is very English, and Italy's noble classicism was turned into a very intimate style. The Georgian style is basically simple. All houses have the same width, all are three stories high, the windows are set functionally. Only the middle storey – the *piano nobile* – is more prominent. There are few ornaments.

Nash, the *arbiter elegantiarum*, was dead, but eighteenth-century Bath remained elegant and fashionable. Society had moved to the upper part of the town, and there were well dressed gentlemen who went to the Assembly Rooms to see the people there. Samuel Johnson and Mrs Thrale also liked to visit the Rooms. Fanny Burney remarked that she never went to look at the people 'who are only seen by going to the Rooms, which we never do'.

Bath became a musically-minded city. There were concerts; Thomas Linley (his daughter Elizabeth later became Mrs Richard Sheridan) conducted a small orchestra at the New Rooms. The oratorios of Handel were performed at the Octagon Proprietary Chapel in Milsom Street. Thomas Gainsborough spent fourteen years at his sister's home (17 The Circus) and met many musicians and actors there, among them Garrick, Henderson and Sarah Siddons. He also met many members of London society. Mrs Elizabeth Montague gave elegant literary parties at her house in the Royal Crescent.

The city was still expanding to the north and to the east. Robert Adam designed Pulteney Bridge, which linked the old town with the Bathwick area across the river. Pulteney Street was later completed according to his designs. Much decorative ironwork remains in some of the eighteenth-century houses, such as the oil lamp standards that face the doorways in Lansdown Crescent.

During the nineteenth century there was a gradual change. The town became a place where people went to live: admirals and generals, lawyers and members of the clergy. This was the society which Jane Austen observed so well. And the city also continued to attract prominent writers and painters. Thomas Carlyle lived with Walter Savage Landor in Rivers Street. He liked the city, 'enclosed amid gnarled, beautifully green and feathered hills'. Landor liked the fact that one could live there on £1,200 a year. By the turn of this century, Bath had become a provincial town with a great tradition. Coal came from the Somerset coal fields, and also stone and iron ore. The Kennet and Avon Canal that linked Bath to Reading was not used much. It had been built in 1810 but it had no chance against the railway. In 1962 a trust was formed to restore the Canal. The locks have been repaired, the water cleared, and boats now carry passengers there.

In 1878, while an engineer was investigating a leak from the King's Bath, the Roman reservoir was discovered, and later the former Roman baths.

Pulteney Bridge, named after Sir William Pulteney of Bath, was designed by Robert Adam. It was originally to be part of a much larger project in which Adam was to have designed a whole street, but Pulteney died before this could be realized and the bridge is the only example of Adam's work in the city.

Excavations began and continued for many years, and now the most important Roman buildings in Britain have been discovered: the pediment of
a vast temple, fine sculptures and carvings, tombstones, jewellery and other
objects which can now be seen in the Roman Baths Museum, where visitors
can feel their way back into the Roman past.

Claverton Manor, a fine country house designed in 1820 by Sir Jeffry
Wyatville, is a good example of the neo-classical style; on 26 July 1897,
Winston Spencer Churchill made his first political speech here. It now
houses the first American Museum established outside the United States,
which was opened in 1961. It aims 'to interpret the history and art of the
United States'. Its story begins with rooms that were occupied two hundred
and fifty years ago by New Englanders. One can study the cultural traditions from the English Puritans to the Spanish colonists of New Mexico.
The work of American craftsmen is shown – silver, pewter, glass, textiles
– and special exhibits are devoted to the American Indian, maritime history, and other aspects of American culture. There is even a replica of
Washington's Mount Vernon Garden, with the octagonal garden house
which was the schoolhouse of George Washington's grandchildren.

'The man who asked for "A Double Scotch" in the Grand Pump Room.' – a watercolour by H. M. Bateman which appeared as a cartoon in *The Tatler* and is now in the Pump Room.

Bath is still popular with tourists, but somehow it remains a museum, though an elegant one. During the Second World War, the Admiralty came to Bath. Bath now has some 50,000 people, the Victorian Art Gallery, a new university opened in 1966, a research institute of the Admiralty, good restaurants, and the usual traffic jams. There are also problems. Will some of the charming Georgian houses be pulled down to make space for late twentieth-century skyscrapers made of concrete and glass? A great many people seem to think that Bath should remain a jewel of the past. Should Bath be a festival city, or a city of industry? We know what the Woods, Robert Adam and Ralph Allen would have said. But they are no longer here. There is much talk in Bath about the quality of life. The waters are still taken 'by elderly colonels and maiden-aunts who also visit Aix-les-Bains and Baden-Baden'. But it all has a *démodé* flavour, and modern guide-books explain that there are also the pleasures of shopping, supermarkets and department stores, pre-London runs of new plays, facilities for all sports, good restaurants such as Popjoy's in what was Beau Nash's house.

If you want to enjoy the old Bath, the beautiful Georgian city, a corner of elegant Old England, it would be better to go there now before Bath becomes too modern.

Brighton

A caricature portrait of George IV by
Gillray, 1792. As Prince Regent and
King he presided over an era of lavish
eating, drinking and gambling. He
visited Brighton for the seawater cure
and transformed the small fishing
village into a popular resort, and it
was here that he commissioned the
exotic palace, Brighton Pavilion.

Shortly before April Fools' Day, 1970, harassed newspaper readers all over the world were delighted by an item from Ye Eccentric Olde England. Owing to the energetic intervention of Sir Laurence Olivier (now Lord Olivier), kippers had been put back on the menu of the *Brighton Belle*, from which they had been wiped off, 'in an outburst of insanity', by some railway executives.

'Not even when nightly strangling Desdemona at the National Theatre did Sir Laurence act to more noble purpose', wrote Collie Knox, a member of the Garrick Club, to the *Daily Telegraph*. *The Times* reported that Olivier had received the telegram, 'We rejoice that you're celebrating Yom Kipper with us this year'. That was the first time I heard about the *Brighton Belle*, an all-Pullman train that ran up and down between London's Victoria Station and Brighton, with pink lampshades on every table.

It was unique and as English as scrambled eggs and kippers, Stilton cheese and port. It no longer exists; a few years ago the *Brighton Belle* became a victim of what is known as progress and modern life. But in a book dedicated to the pleasure of the past, the *Brighton Belle* must be mentioned. In scope, speed, and streamlining the *Belle* could not compare with France's *Mistral*, the Trans-European-Express trains in Germany or Switzerland's light-metal trains; but it was much nicer. It made the fifty-five-mile trip from Victoria to Brighton in fifty-five minutes.

Compared with the Wagon-Lits' royal-blue coaches, the much smaller blue-grey Pullmans of British Rail, with the white inscription *Brighton Belle*, looked like toy cars. The train consisted of two half-trains, each made up of two first-class Pullman carriages (twenty seats) and three second-class cars (forty-eight to fifty-six seats). The first-class cars had ladies' names: Doris and Hazel, Audrey and Vera, Mona and Gwen. Nearly everybody aboard the *Brighton Belle* was a habitué, and nearly every habitué had his favourite car.

I travelled from Victoria to Brighton on the eleven o'clock morning train in Hazel because it had a non-smoking compartment. Doris, next to it, was smoking only. Victoria Station, grey and grimy, was as awful as ever, but something happened the moment I stepped through Gate 14 with its small blue-white shield, 'Brighton Belle'. An aristocratic conductor, possibly on loan from Claridge's, greeted me genially, as the older staff members at Claridge's greet royalty and ex-royalty. I was later told that several *Brighton Belle* conductors did occasionally serve on Her Majesty's Royal Car.

As I stepped into the wood-panelled Pullman, there was the unmistakable atmosphere of an old, exclusive club. Reddish mahogany walls with inlaid ornaments, a dark-yellow rug with brown stripes, charcoal-and-grey checked armchairs with white headrests and the word 'Pullman', two chairs with each table. In the second class, four people would sit around a table.

White tablecloth, old silver inscribed with the words 'Pullman Car Company Limited', and Staffordshire china. All very Victorian, including a couple of ladies who reminded me of the late Agatha Christie's Miss Marple.

The steward's name was Francis Tindell. He had been a Pullman car steward for the past thirty-five years.

'A little longer than the age of this car,' he said, letting his fingers glide over the panelling in a tender gesture. 'She's thirty-three, and still keeping up, isn't she, sir?'

I agreed. It wouldn't be nice to say, 'Yes but how long will she last?' Precisely at eleven o'clock the train left Victoria and immediately picked up speed. Another suburban train crowded with second-class passengers was running parallel. Some people stared at us in awe, and one man photographed the *Brighton Belle* through his window. The other train didn't look very nice, and probably wasn't. Many people now complain about many British trains since the railways were nationalized. Anthony Sampson called them 'the most embarrassing of all Britain's Victorian left-overs'.

Though the *Brighton Belle* looked like an improbable museum piece, it was not old, dating only from 1933. The Brighton line is much older though. The first train left London for Brighton on 19 September 1841. 'Church bells rang out the good news and fireworks blazed in the sky.' It took two

A nineteenth-century engraving showing the Chain Pier and sea promenade.

hours to get to Brighton, quite an improvement after the former six-hour coach service. First-class rail fare was fourteen shillings and sixpence. (I paid the equivalent of three dollars with a sixty-cent supplement for Pullman). No refreshments were served until the first Pullman car arrived in 1875. There was a strict no-smoking rule in the carriages and at station stops along the line. Foot warmers could be hired for sixpence, whenever the train's heating failed to meet the requirements of passengers. A glass of water was provided at each station en route.

'The elite of the nineteenth century were able to travel south in comfort in trains which were composed of first-class carriages and the working

The *Southern Belle* is renamed the *Brighton Belle* at Victoria Station in 1933.

population enjoyed the cheap day-return from London to the sea', wrote chronicler Reg Moore. The Brighton line also shortened the journey from London to Paris. Steam packets sailed regularly from Brighton to Dieppe in France; the London–Paris trip took only half a day. It may take longer today by air, with long waits at the airport.

In 1933, the line was electrified. An all-Pullman train, originally called the *Southern Belle*, was put into service. Another Pullman train, the *Bournemouth Belle*, connected Waterloo Station with the famous Hampshire resort. That train no longer exists either. All the *Belles* are gone. The staff had no illusion.

'Some day soon our lovely carriages will fall to pieces,' said Mr John Verrall, the conductor. 'In addition to the ten cars on this train there are five more at the Brighton depot, and they are just as old. It's only a question of time. Too bad, really, since trains all over the world are deficit operations yet the *Brighton Belle* is making money. Modern air-conditioned Pullman cars would probably pay off. More people than before dislike to drive their cars down to the coast.'

Mr Verrall said that until a few years ago the *Brighton Belle* had been operated by the Pullman Company, a private outfit. He had worn a more elegant uniform with gold braid. Service was grand, as good as in the finest hotels. Everything was served on silver and green-gold china. There was a terrific wine list. Mr Verrall permitted himself an inaudible sigh.

Later Mr Tindell served tea. The teapot was not old silver, but made of some shiny metal, with the inscription, 'British Rail'. The tea was fine though. Mr Tindell left after surveying the table – tea, hot water, milk, lemon, sugar. Everything in place.

Mr Verrall said that each run of the *Brighton Belle* had a different atmosphere. 'We start out in the morning in Brighton where the staff lives. On the morning trip there are businessmen and ladies going to London to do their shopping. Many have breakfast on the train.'

'Scrambled eggs and kippers?'

'Yes, certainly. On the eleven o'clock, from London to Brighton, we have sunshine seekers during the warm-weather period. On the twelve-forty-five, from Brighton to London, there are more businessmen, having lunch on the train. The two-o'clock departure form Victoria is somewhat in-between. Theatre-goers and performers take the five-forty-five from Brighton, which gets into Victoria at six-forty. At seven many businessmen return to Brighton, having drinks on the train before going home for dinner. The eight-forty-five from Brighton is always crowded in summertime when the sunshine seekers go home. But the eleven-o'clock from Victoria is the best run of all, if I may say so. The performers and the impresarios go home. There may be lots of champagne if the new show was a success. This run can be *quite* gay.' On the *Brighton Belle* one could get a drink even when the pubs were closed. The licensing laws don't apply to the train 'while in motion'.

Brighton has become popular with theatre people who escape from The Big Smoke to the beach where they live all year round in houses and apartments. The 'kipper affair' listed some of the then prominent habitués of the *Belle*; Olivier, Dame Flora Robson, Anna Neagle, Sir John Clements, Paul Scofield, Alan Melville.

Mr Ronald Simpson, the chef de cuisine on our train, a competent man of sixty, said he could serve 192 people in five cars breakfast, lunch, dinner, or supper, which took some doing since the journey lasted less than an hour. The train was often sold out, and there were 384 people on it, but the staff of fourteen (plus conductor and engineer) was able to manage. The kitchen was a model of compactness and organization, no larger than a comfortable clothes closet. There was a small range, an electric grill, a small table, the sink. Mr Simpson kept fish (kippers and halibut), sirloin steak, ham, cheese, butter, salad, and other staples in a small refrigerator. The menu featured a soup of the day, eggs styled to choice, Welsh rabbit, grilled kippers, fried fillet of halibut, grilled sirloin at very moderate prices. If the chef was not too busy, he would make an omelet for an habitué, or other dishes that were not on the menu. And there were cold things and sandwiches.

The wine list, 'no longer what it used to be, sir', was amazing. Champagne, two clarets, a white Bordeaux, two red Burgundies, two rosés, a Pouilly-Fuissé, the inevitable Liebfraumilch, a Zeltinger Riesling, an Alsatian wine, four sherries, a dozen spirits and liqueurs, half a dozen different beers, cider, mineral waters, fruit juices, and Pepsi Cola. The *Brighton Belle* was perfect for going to Brighton. It was a train of the past – and Brighton, after all, is a place of the past.

Brighton is certainly bizarre. The railroad station was financed by David Mocatta. Built in 'early Italian style', whatever than means, it resembles an Oriental palace and would be a sensation in Southern California. The station was erected on an artificial plateau cut out of the steep slopes of Dyke Road, with an arcade in front and a colonnade around, and was lighted at night by several hundred gas burners. It cost only twelve thousand pounds – a bargain. Three and a half million people use it every year.

The 1866 edition of Baedeker's *London* says, 'Brighton, the most popular resort near London, was until 1782 a poor fishing village. Once it was called Brighthelmstone. It is certain that the Romans had been here. In the eleventh century, the land belonged to Lord Godwin, the father of King

Brighton Station and Dyke Road, 1841. The Station colonnade continues around the building and it was once lit at night by several hundred gas burners.

Harold who lost his life and land in the Battle of Hastings . . . In 1782, George IV (then the Prince of Wales) had the Royal Pavilion built, a big, ugly structure in Oriental style where he later spent several months every year. Queen Victoria often lived there. Since 1851, the Brighton Pavilion belongs to the city, which often uses it for public functions.'

The Royal Brighton Pavilion is still there, so monumentally ugly that it is fascinating. Originally designed in the 'Hindustan style', it was completed by John Nash in 1822. It is very popular with visitors who consider it enchanting though they do not quite know how it fits in. They have learned that Brighton's golden age was the Regency, the period lasting from 1811 to 1820, when George, Prince of Wales (later George IV) acted for his father, George III. It was an age of elegant naughtiness and aristocratic eccentricity. The fat Regent was never as popular as, say, Charles II. He looked impossible and wore a corset. But he presided over an era that is dear to the hearts of many English for its drinking, gambling and hell-raising, and it happened mostly in Brighton.

The Pavilion reflects none of the English 'Regency Style'. No striped satin papers, gold-and-white striped fabrics, no blue ceilings with gold stars.

Instead the ceilings of the Pavilion show dragons and serpents, there is an organ in the music rooms, there are glass chandeliers. Probably the most popular room in the Pavilion is the kitchen with rows of dummy joints of meat and a spit where a whole dummy ox is turned on the spit. As one walks through the rooms, one hears the quiet sounds of music, string quartets by Haydn and Mozart. But the Royal Pavilion remains one of the great houses of England and will always be popular.

Brighton's most interesting period, however, was not the Regency, but the earlier time from 1750 to 1790, when it became the healing spring for the hypochondriacs of London. Two doctors, Dr Richard Russell and his successor, Dr Anthony Relhan, discovered that sea water might cure hydrophobia and many other ills. Brighton was still a village, but elegant people went there, when Dr Russell explained to them, that bathing in the sea would cure the ills that too much gin, too much food and too cold air had caused. Sea bathing was no pleasure and was not meant to be. In the month of November, 1782, Fanny Burney, the novelist, swam for her life – more exactly, for her health – in the cold sea water in the company of Mrs Thrale, the friend of Samuel Johnson. It must have been terrible. Decorum was preserved by having ladies and gentlemen swimming in different parts of the beach; gentlemen used telescopes to look at the ladies, at least the guidebooks said so. As in all other spas, the doctors' orders had to be followed. The poor people not only were told to swim in the cold water, preferably at dawn, but also to drink the terrible sea water. The successor of Dr Relhan, a certain Dr Awsiter, wrote, 'To remove the loathing, sickness and thirst, with which sea water, taken pure, is always attended, it should be mixed with an equal quantity of new milk. Thus it becomes a noble medicine.'

When the Regent and his court arrived in the late 1780s, the 'sick' people were politely told to get out, because the Regent was full of life and had no wish to see 'sick' people. But Brighton had become an important spa, offering springs called 'stromboli' and Turkish baths called 'shampoos'. Imitations of the better known German spa treatments were also offered.

opposite The Royal Pavilion in Brighton, an exotic piece of architecture in oriental style commissioned by the Prince Regent in 1782.

overleaf The Old Pavilion and Steyne from an engraving by C. Richards of Brighton in 1806.

above Fanny Burney, the novelist, who bathed for her health at Brighton during the winter of 1782.

below Sunday morning on the lawn in 1879. Fashionable promenaders would regularly 'take the air' along the sea front.

A certain Mr Nathan Smith had an air pump with which he was able 'to extract gout'. In 1811 a local blacksmith was able to relieve the Regent's toothache by directing hot smoke into the Regent's mouth. Around the middle of the century there were warm sea-water baths in Brighton that were said to cure many ills.

The Regent was gone, the court had left, and the Pavilion was already considered a monstrosity, but the Regency style was there to stay. It is still there in railings, balconies and street lamps along King's Road facing the sea. The lamps have small crowns. Garlands of coloured lights are strung up everywhere, wound even around the street-lights. It must have been quite a place during the Belle Epoque. In Brighton the usually privacy-conscious English gather for togetherness. On warm summer days, tens of thousands are gathered, even crowded, next to each other on the beach, in Coney Island style, with transistor radios, while half a mile away the beach is blissfully empty.

The important hotels are along King's Road, the sea promenade. The Grand, already praised by Baedeker in 1866, is still there, quiet and somehow rich, with many columns and art nouveau ornaments. Both the Tories and the Labour Party come here for their annual 'conferences'. Flamboyant people, colonels and bookmakers are said to go to the Metropole. Nearby are the racecourses of Goodwood and Kemp Town, several golf courses, bowling alleys, skating rinks, dozens of cinemas, and delightful walks on the rolling South Downs. There is the famed Theatre Royal where many plays have made their pre-London run. There are strange shops offering their goods such as Ye Olde Fashion Humbugge Shoppe, and there are lovely pubs.

It is said that Brighton is the rendezvous of illicit lovers, the underworld, the sporting world, and of suburban holidaymakers. It also has a fine collection of fortune-tellers – crystal-gazers, palmists and all sorts of mediums – who make Brighton a first rate spa for contemporary hypochondriacs and naïve believers, just as it once was the place for people who believed that sea water would cure all ills. All spas exist only as long as people believe in them, and judging by the crowds, people still believe in Brighton.

There are still fine old houses, terraces and squares along the King's Road, in the Regency style which remained alive when elsewhere in England the Victorian style dominated architecture. A whole town, Kemp Town, built in the Regency style, fell into decay and became a slum. It was re-discovered like Pimlico in London and the Marais district in Paris. It is certainly an incredible place and has to be seen to be believed.

That also goes for the Lanes, an intricate labyrinth of narrow alleys with bookstores, boutiques, antique and pseudo-antique shops where one gets pleasantly lost. Once the Lanes were a source of widespread curiosity and

opposite The Friedrichsbad cloister in Baden-Baden. The Friedrichsbad, the Ducal bathing establishment, is to the left of the picture and the New Castle, now a museum, towers above the steps.

business was said to be excellent there. Much of the things offered seem pure junk but if you have patience and perseverance you may find a beautiful old clock there, a brass piece, an ancient print, each genuine and perhaps even worth its price if you do not mind haggling a little. Brighton has been called an English microcosm because it still shows different ways of living. Today businessmen, stockbrokers, bankers, stage people live there all year round.

Brighton has survived its reputation as a naughty place where one could meet 'the frail daughters of Venus'. The daughters, not frail anymore, now promenade the fashionable streets of London. But Brighton reflects English history for the past two hundred years. Visitors promenading along King's Road may even feel as if they were in Thackeray's *Vanity Fair*. A certain naughty note, that was revived by the inimitable Prince of Wales who later became Edward VII seems to stick to Brighton in the minds of many English. Brighton is no longer naughty, not in our day. But it remains a fascinating mirror of a past English life.

Brighton today faces an uncertain future. As so many other places with a great past, it finds itself at the crossroads. Should Brighton give up its beautiful, though sometimes outrageous past and become 'a disaster in concrete'? The danger signals are there.

There exists the menu of a luncheon which the great Marie-Antoine (Antonin) Carême, the founder of the classic French *grande cuisine*, prepared one day in January, 1817, for the Prince Regent and forty guests. It has to be seen to be believed, it is wonderful and vulgar, as so many other things in Brighton, but today it seems mostly wonderful.

The menu begins with eight soups, among them a *tortue au vin de Madère*, continues with eight fish dishes (*le turbot grillé sauce aux huîtres, le saumon à la Génoise*) continues with forty-two, yes, forty-two entrées (*de petits soufflés de volaille et de gibier, le turban de filets mignons à l'écarlate*), eight different roasts, forty entremets (*les truffes à l'italienne, les oeufs à la Bretonne*), and much, much later – there were 124 different dishes – you could finish with *fondue au Parmesan* or *petits soufflés à l'orange*. All these delicacies were served at the same time and the lunch must have been as incredible as the Royal Pavilion in Brighton, where it was served. The guests had problems though. If they were seated at the end of the table, they had to eat *les filets de canards*, which were served there while the lucky people at the head of the table were offered *escaloppes de faisans aux truffes de France*.

The confusion must have been Brightonian, and this was a long time before the invention of Alka-Seltzer. Yet the Prince Regent loved it, and tomorrow there would be another terrific meal. He did not mind the *service à la française*, the simultaneous presentation of many dishes. He assured Carême that he found his cooking 'easy to digest'. The great

The Royal Pavilion, a fantasy palace commissioned by the Prince Regent, which was completed by Nash in 1820. The exotic exterior was inspired by Indian architecture whereas the interior, notably the Banqueting Room, reflects the Regent's extravagant tastes in Chinese art.

left The Royal Crescent. One of the few terraces in Brighton with a brick façade.

below The North side of Sussex Square, in Kemp Town, showing the Regency-style terraces.

George Auguste Escoffier, who became Carême's successor as the great reformer of the *grande cuisine*, wrote, 'Carême had grasped the essential truth that the richer cooking is, the more speedily do the stomach and palate tire of it.'

All this happened in Brighton, not in a sunny corner of France. No wonder that there are still people in the spa who speak about 'Prinny', the Prince Regent, as though he were still around, and are deeply shocked by the efforts of the urban planners. Ah, where are the times when the Prince Regent lived with his wife *and* with Mrs Fitzherbert, under the same roof, and when permissiveness existed in Brighton while the rest of England did not know the meaning of the word? When John Nash and Robert Jones worked hard to make the Royal Pavilion even more incredible, when Charles Busby and Amon Wilds created their crazy and beautiful Regency façades. Where but in Brighton could there be a place like Brunswick Square, with a small palatial buildings facing the sea? Even Prince Metternich spoke highly of Brighton.

It is true that Queen Victoria never liked the place and stayed at the Pavilion only until 1845. She said she was getting tired of all these people around staring at her. Five years later the Royal Pavilion was sold to the city of Brighton for a lousy 53,000 pounds. Ironically, everybody thereafter began to build in Victorian style, and Sir Osbert Sitwell later complained that Brighton had become the victim of Victorian elephantiasis.

Somehow Brighton survived and now keeps up a way of life between the old Regency and Victorian styles and the new non-styles that one sees around Rank Centre and Churchill Square. That is probably known as progress, but it should not have happened to Brighton. Fortunately the Palace Pier is still there, and seven million people come every year to enjoy the restaurants and attractions, promenades and gambling establishments. Most people come in November, when the weather is almost always bad, to watch the Brighton Rally.

Perhaps the visitors come for other reasons too. They want to see the place where London's High Society once came for fun. Where as late as 1950 executives would take their secretaries for the weekend. A ticket on the *Brighton Belle* was a ticket for a 'dirty weekend', or a glorious adventure.

The *Brighton Belle* is gone, and a way of life, but Brighton is still there, with its Lanes, old pubs, lunch at the English Oyster Bar and Wheeler's, the lovely façades and the memories of yesterday. The Royal Pavilion is still there, and some people will wonder how such things could happen. As I said before, seeing is believing. I do hope Brighton will essentially remain the Brighton of the past, the Brighton that 'Prinny' created.

Baden-Baden

Looking over the town of Baden-
Baden from the Neues Schloss, with a
view of the Black Forest behind.

Baden-Baden remains indestructible. After two world wars and assorted disasters that have broken the elegant backbone of many of Europe's fine resorts, Baden-Baden is still Germany's most famous spa, a showplace of feudal grandeur and noble detachment. The double name served after 1535 to distinguish the two margravial lines of Baden-Baden and Baden-Durlach, and survived after their reunion in 1771. It now serves to distinguish the elegant spa from the less elegant Baden near Vienna and Baden near Zürich, not elegant at all. The great Aubusson in the baroque gambling hall is said to be the finest in the world. The Casino is the most ornate in Europe and Germany's oldest gambling establishment.

The Casino was built in 1821 from Friedrich Weinbrenner's design when it replaced the 'promenade house' of 1766. Business was slow at first and picked up only at the time of the Congress of Vienna. Located halfway between Paris and Vienna, and between Russia and Spain, Baden-Baden became a favourite stopping-off place for diplomats and dukes. Many stayed on for months, spending plenty. Baden-Baden's lucky break came in 1832 when a campaign against gambling started in England. Six years later, Louis-Philippe of France closed all French gambling houses, including the Palais Royal in Paris. He could not stop the gamblers from gambling though. Frenchmen began to look for a convenient place to lose their money. They found it on the east bank of the Rhine, in Baden-Baden, already known as 'Europe's summer capital'.

With the gamblers came Jacques Bénazet, a fabulous entrepreneur who had been leasee of the Palais Royal. He understood that a gambling casino needs more than roulette tables: there must be beautiful women, good food and good wines, entertainment and well-kept parks to make unhappy losers forget the previous night's heavy losses. Baden-Baden had everything – perfect scenery, a perfect climate and a near-perfect history. It was a cosmopolitan synthesis of Gallic *esprit* and German *Gemütlichkeit*. Only the Rhine separates German Rieslings from French Rieslings.

Jacques Bénazet, now known as the uncrowned King of Baden-Baden, and his son, Edouard, 'Le Duc de Zéro', fell in love with Baden-Baden. They invested large sums of money and did things in a big way. They found an enthusiastic ally in the Grand-Duchess, née Stéphanie de Beauharnais, an adopted daughter of Napoleon Bonaparte, and a lady with ardent social ambitions. The Bénazets rebuilt the shabby casino into an imitation Versailles. The four main rooms were decorated by the theatrical designers of the Paris Opéra. All styles from Renaissance to Empire are represented in the gambling halls. There is a winter garden with fancy fountains and the 'white' hall in Louis XVI style; the 'red' hall (Louis XIV) that once served as the stage for intimate theatre performances; the 'Salon Pompadour' or 'yellow' hall (Louis XV) with a charming Marly-and-Trianon imitation;

An engraving of one of the gambling halls of the Casino built by the Bénazets in the early nineteenth century. It was decorated by theatrical designers of the Paris Opéra.

and behind is the 'green' hall (Louis XIII) which was formerly used as a grand ballroom. Purists may be shocked by the architectural mish-mash of styles but among Europe's gambling casinos, some of which have trouble keeping up a respectable appearance, Baden-Baden is a gem – though an imitation gem, to be sure.

After the foundation of the German Empire in 1870 gaming was forbidden by law and all German gambling houses were ordered to close. Baden-Baden's poison became Monte Carlo's meat. This time the French casinos prospered as the international brotherhood of big-time gamblers migrated back across the Rhine. For more than sixty years, the little ivory ball no longer span in Baden-Baden. On 3 October 1933 the Nazis reopened the Casino. Not because they liked gambling but they needed the hard currency the gamblers would bring. The Depression had wiped out promising sources of cash however, and many gamblers did not like the martial characters with sabre scars and their peroxide-blonde *Damen* across the roulette tables. In 1944 the Casino was closed again. It was reopened on 1 April 1950, by special permission of the French occupation authorities.

The Bénazets would approve of the Casino if they could see it today. It is larger, brighter, more elegant than ever. Roulette, baccarat and black jack are played, roulette from 2 p.m. to 2 a.m., baccarat until 7 a.m. Anybody over twenty-one may gamble; except local residents or students. In the past few years the bank has been broken several times. Unlike Monte Carlo, the table in Baden-Baden is not covered with a black cloth while new funds are fetched. The money is brought in and the croupier calls, '*Bitte das Spiel zu machen*'.

The Friedrichsbad from an engraving of 1889. It was built after the gambling halls, then the main attraction, had been closed. The hottest springs in Europe supply the water for the baths.

Baden-Baden's second great attraction is its baths, much older than the gambling halls. The Romans discovered the thermal springs of Aquae Aureliae two thousand years ago. Emperor Caracalla (211–217) personally laid out the rather undemocratic local baths, whose designs can be seen in the catacombs below the Römerplatz. At the bottom were the baths used by Roman G.I.s; above them were those of the officers; on top were the imperial baths used by the emperors. Theophrastus Paracelsus, the sixteenth-century medical practitioner, wrote in 1541, 'So that the sick people may be cured, the Lord has ruled in His Creation that more strength be found in springs than in learned prescriptions. And the hot springs of Badin (*sic*) are more perfect than anything else.'

The hot springs of Baden-Baden, north-east of the Stiftskirche, come from a depth of some 6500 feet and they are the hottest in Europe. The most famous are Friedrichs Spring (151°F.), Hell Spring (155°F.) and Cool Spring, one of the 'coldest', 131°F. All are radioactive; Mur Spring contains 60·7 Mache units of radon. Others are Cloister Spring, Brüh Spring, Jew Spring; there are about twenty of them. They are united into two conduits, the Hauptstollen and the Kirchenstollen, and are conducted to the bathhouses and drinking establishments.

The Friedrichsbad was built in 1869 and opened in 1877, when the gambling halls had been closed, and Baden-Baden was reviving its reputation as a medical spa. It was modernized, completely overhauled after the last war and now contains more machines and apparatus than a good-sized factory. It offers innumerable variations of hot and cold baths. Over a hundred years ago, a German clergyman named Kneipp preached the gospel of hydrotherapy. Water, he said, would cure practically every disease. Kneipp's enthusiastic followers, of whom there are legions in Europe, consider Baden-Baden's Friedrichsbad their mecca. Water from the hot springs is said to be an excellent treatment for arthritis, neuralgia and respiratory diseases. In the Trinkhalle (Pump Room), built around 1840, with sixteen Corinthian columns and slabs of pale-brown terracotta, tired Europeans 'take the waters'. The exact amount of water to be taken, and when, its temperature, and other significant details are prescribed by a member of that venerable European fraternity, the *Kurarzt*. The spa doctor's word is law. He not only tells you when and what to drink, what you may eat, he also intimates, with just the faintest frown, that he will receive 'reports' on you, presumably from waiters, chambermaids and assorted informers. Better watch your step. Of course, the cure can be fun, 'if you co-operate'.

The modern bathhouse is the Augustabad, built in the 1960s, replacing the original baths of 1887. It is located behind the former Convent of the Holy Sepulchre that was founded in 1670 by the Margravine Maria Franziska.

left The arcaded entrance to the Trinkhalle (Pump Room) showing the frescoes and terracotta tiles which decorate the walls.

below Kaiser Wilhelm I, who became German emperor in 1871. He visited Baden-Baden every summer with twelve horses, twelve coachmen and a small entourage.

The main building with the large reception hall has seven storeys. All the treatments available in Baden-Baden are found here: tub baths with specialized and cold-water treatment, mud packs, an inhalatorium, fountain galleries, a mineral water swimming pool (56 feet by 26 feet), and sun-bathing terraces. There are two anti-stress plans, Anti-Stress I (with medical supervision) and Anti-Stress II (without medical supervision), in case the sight of a doctor causes you stress. A brochure informs you that Baden-Baden is completely equipped for the treatment of stress, and who does not suffer from stress these days? Facilities also exist for the treatment of general fatigue and exhaustion, not to mention cardiac and circulatory problems, metabolic disorders, respiratory diseases. Apparently there is no disease that cannot be treated in Baden-Baden.

Europeans are enthusiastic spa-visitors. They believe firmly that there is a spa for every ill in the book. Veterans of other spas claim that the doctors of Baden-Baden are more reasonable than their colleagues elsewhere. They attribute this mildness to the mild climate and the mild landscape of Baden-Baden. Actually, the cure is rarely a reason for going to Baden-Baden. Often it is only a pretext for having a few weeks of fun and relaxation. The day in Baden-Baden begins with the patients' private chauffeurs washing the limousines in front of the hotels, and it ends with the owners of the limousines losing a little money at the Casino. Gambling is not forbidden by the spa doctors, neither is it encouraged.

Nothing ever changes here, that is the greatest attraction of the place. At Brenner's Park Hotel, well-heeled guests walk softly across the beautiful, large Isfahan rug in the lobby that was already admired by their well-heeled fathers and grandfathers. Blue-white signs saying KURGEBIET (resort area) separate the plebeian city of Baden-Baden (all-year-round population circa 49,000) with its noisy traffic and plain citizens from the silent, tree-shaded section with its Casino and hotels, its de luxe suites and expensive guests. Even without the signs, the division between the two worlds would be obvious. The *Kurverwaltung* (spa administration) is trying hard to preserve the resort's *fin de siècle* cachet. The people know that the guests love Baden-Baden and come back there because it has not changed. The present-day guests insist that nothing must be altered. Non-change can be very expensive. When the draperies must be changed because they are torn, they must have the same old draperies made which costs money.

Those were the days. Taxes were a joke, and wealth was a state of mind, taken for granted. You could walk down Lichtentaler Allee in the morning and you would meet Queen Victoria, Kaiser Wilhelm I and Tsar Alexander II. The Kaiser and the Tsar lived in splendour, but Queen Victoria occupied three austere rooms in the home of her relative, Prince von Hohenlohe, a modest wooden house in Capucins' Street, not the very best

An engraving of Baden-Baden in the late 1880s.

neighbourhood. The natives loved her for her modesty. Like the people of Boston, they hate to show off. The thing here is to conceal one's wealth. The great old villas in Baden-Baden are surrounded by thick walls and old parks that screen off the treasures within.

Years ago the spa administration, in a desperate effort to re-create the charm of the past, transferred the old lanterns from the mediaeval part of the town to the resort area. The illusion of the past must be kept alive. A very old gentleman, who has been in Baden-Baden many times since the turn of the century, told me that nothing had been changed here, thank God. The resort is still one vast English park, with some of the most beautiful lawns south of the British Isles, and with exotic trees carefully planted to convey a sense of elegant disorder. Trees were imported from America, China, Japan, Greece and Spain. There are red New England maples and weeping beeches and old sequoias. The Allee is so beautiful that the local peasants used to dress up when they had to walk through. Baden-Baden blends effortlessly into the surrounding landscape, the dark woodlands and softly rounded hills of the Black Forest, better known as Schwarzwald.

'If you have to live to be over ninety in this world of ours,' the old gentleman said philosophically, 'I suppose this place is the place to try it.'

A crystal-clear, little stream, the Oos (pronounced 'Oh's'), flows down the lovely green valley. Once it was the historic boundary between the Franconian tribes on the west and the Alemans on the east, and between the bishoprics of Speyer and Strasbourg. The nuns of the Cistercian convent wanted to be in the domain of the bishop of Speyer, so one day they simply altered the course of the Oos. It still makes a band around the land that belonged to the convent. Pretty little bridges lead across the stream into well-kept hotel gardens, with signs informing the intruder that 'entrance is allowed only to our guests'. And everywhere there are the old trees.

'Come to Baden-Baden', Turgenev wrote to Flaubert, 'there are trees here such as I've never seen elsewhere.'

In Baden-Baden, the trees are a state of mind. Nowadays anybody with plenty of money can build tennis courts, a golf course, swimming pools, large hotels, even a Kurhaus. But can they build one-hundred-year-old, rare trees?

There *are* tennis courts, golf courses, large hotels, a race track, and a Kurhaus in Baden-Baden. And above all, there are the trees. In the park of the Villa Ruschawey I copied the names of some of them from small metal plates on the trunks: *Acer palmatum atropurpureum* (China), *Liriodendron tulipifera* (America), *Cedrus atlantica* (Africa), *Picea Abies* (Lapland), *Fagus silvatica purpurea* (Caucasus), *Castanea sativa* (South Africa). There was even a 'make-believe' acacia which seemed to thrive in the make-believe climate of Baden-Baden where the winters are mild and the summers are velvety, and spring and autumn are said to be heaven. Each tree has its case history, like a patient in a hospital, and many must not be tampered with without official permission. And among the old trees stand old houses filled with old art treasures, still owned by the old families who built them a hundred years ago and who have managed to survive depressions and taxes and inflation.

Along the Oos there is an old-fashioned tulip-and-rose garden, with carefully clipped hedges, flower beds and ornamental columns that would be outrageous elsewhere but look just right here. It is true that some of the old villas had to be turned into pensions, and one fine castle was bought by the Federal Railroads and became a vacation home for tired conductors. But this is as far as Baden-Baden will admit welfare-state recreation. Sometimes the expensive hotels – and they are very expensive – are sold out and there are still rooms in the modest ones. According to the Spring 1979 list, a double room at Brenner's Park Hotel may be over 260 marks, but in a small place two people can live in a room for 40 marks. It is doubtful though whether Baden-Baden will lose its reputation of being Germany's most expensive resort and spa.

Will they be able to preserve the spirit of nostalgia? The danger signals are up. The Lichtentaler Allee where once emperors went horseback riding before breakfast and mad Russian grand-dukes drove their troikas after midnight, has been paved with asphalt and has become a racetrack for French jeeps. This seems to have injured the roots of some beautiful old oaks for many of them are said to be dying. A few years ago, *Badisches Tagblatt*, the local paper, reprinted an ancient police ordinance of 19 July 1838:

'There have been several protests against fast riding and driving . . . The police decrees that as of today horseback riders and coachmen must reduce their speed.'

So far there has been no success. The hotel parking lots are filled with vulgar, chauffeur-driven Mercedes 600s and Rolls-Royces. An East German newspaper reported that 'In the streets of Baden-Baden, where a day costs as much as the weekly income of a German worker, the snobs of the West move on with lazy gestures . . . ' Obviously, the reporter was not there on a recent weekend when the gravelled paths and well-mown lawns were crowded with what the resort management calls *Kurschrecks* (resort terrors) – noisy citizens with strangely shaped straw hats, wearing their shirts outside their trousers, eating *wurst* and drinking beer, sitting under the branches of a weeping beech, and throwing empty bottles and greasy paper all over the place. It was quite a shock for the spa management. For a while they put up posters showing a *Kurschreck* who holds a mirror in his hand. *Kurschrecks* who do not like to see themselves in these mirrors have torn down some of the posters. The spa management continues its crusade against noise and vulgarity and advertises Baden-Baden as the Queen of the Black Forest, with its 'bewitching spell of the remains of ancient history'.

The Casino made enormous profits and the Bénazets kept the money rolling. They built a fine race track in nearby Iffezheim where two important meetings are now held, a Spring Meeting in the second half of May and the six-day International Race Week at the end of August and beginning of September. The Grand Prix of Baden, now 200,000 D-Mark, is a European turf event. They imported French architects and built a baroque theatre in the style of the Paris Opéra, in the Goetheplatz. It was opened by Hector Berlioz who conducted 'Béatrice et Bénédict' there on 9 August 1862, a work especially written for the occasion.

Edouard Bénazet liked to please high- *and* low-brows. He invited the Comédie Française but also the Bouffes Parisiennes, imported dreamy poets with definite talent and beautiful women of uncertain virtue. He tried to make everybody happy. It was said, '*Toutes les rivières vont à la mer et toutes les jolies femmes à Bade.*' When Bénazet wanted to thank a friend for a favour, he gave him a small castle. A century ago, Baden-Baden was the most fashionable resort in the world.

There were scandals galore. A Russian prince was killed by his mistress. Prince Stourdza of Rumania was killed by a group of anarchists disguised as priests. A Polish nobleman, name unknown, broke the bank when 'red' came out thirteen times in a row. Mrs Dostoevsky complained that her husband lost all his earnings at the Casino and was even robbed of his top-coat. In 1866 he wrote 'The Gambler'.

Baden-Baden was said to be finished when all gambling casinos were closed in Germany in 1872, but the resort's reputation survived. Kaiser Wilhelm I (whose bust is now in front of the Trinkhalle) still came every summer and lived at the Hotel Messmer which changed its name to 'Maison Messmer' while he was there. Protocol forbade that the emperor live at a 'hotel'. His Majesty and Kaiserin Augusta came with twelve coachmen, twelve black horses and a small entourage. Nothing was to be changed, and when an old tree threatened to grow into the window of the Kaiser's room, he forbade them to cut it. He went there for forty years, but the place became old-fashioned and eventually disappeared. One of the Messmer daughters, Augusta (the godchild of the Kaiserin Augusta) married a more successful hotel proprietor, Camille Brenner. Another became lady-in-waiting to the Kaiserin at the court in Berlin. Baden-Baden was that kind of place.

Napoleon III lived at the Villa Stephanie, then called the Stephanie les Bains Hotel, later bought by Anton Brenner, a smart court tailor who renamed it Brenner's Hotel Stephanie. The Stephanie was then *the* place

The Trinkhalle, built around 1840. Sixteen Corinthian pillars support the arcade. The bust is of Kaiser Wilhelm I.

to stay. Victoria and Princess Beatrice stayed there, as did the princes of Wales (later Edward VII and George V), the kings of Norway and Sweden, Anastasia of Mecklenburg, Dom Pedro II, and the Emperor of Brazil. Also Prince Otto von Bismarck, King Alfonso XIII of Spain and the Emperor of Siam. That ought to give you the idea.

Back to the scandals. The Duke of Hamilton, paying off a lost bet, once led a calf through Lichtentaler Allee. Count Alexander Potocki was always followed by an old lady who held an umbrella above his head. The rich and new-rich from Russia, France and England went to Baden-Baden to enjoy the company of nobility. The poor rich stayed at the expensive hotels. The rich rich built their own homes. A villa in Baden-Baden became a social must.

The largest houses were built by Russian aristocrats: the Gorchakovs, Trubetzkoys, Menchikovs, Kreptovichs. They even put up a Russian Orthodox church in Byzantine style; it now belongs to the Russian Orthodox diocese in Germany. The sandstone building is surmounted by a blue onion-shaped dome which was originally gilded. The coffee king Siehlken built Villa Mariahalden. The Krupps built not one but two castles. Turgenev ordered a Renaissance villa to be built near Dostoevsky's. Johannes Brahms spent the summers from 1865 to 1874 at Maximilianstrasse 5, where he occupied two attic rooms. It was here that he wrote his Second (Lichtental) Symphony. He would compose in the morning and in the afternoon he would tear up the pages that did not satisfy him. He often walked up to the New Castle to look out across the Rhine plain. On a clear day he might see Strasbourg Cathedral, far in the distance.

Camille Brenner, the afore-mentioned son of the court tailor, became the César Ritz of Baden-Baden. By the turn of the last century the Stephanie was *the* hotel in Germany, a luxurious extravaganza with fifty suites,

Brenner's Parkhotel, 'one of the last truly great hotels in Europe', built by Camille Brenner in the early 1900s.

each furnished differently. Every good room had a private bathroom. Many people predicted that the Brenners would go broke. After all, it was said, even Kaiser Wilhelm I did not have a private bath in his castle in Berlin. On Saturday nights, when the Kaiser wanted a hot bath, he would send to the public bathhouse for a tub. Hard to believe; maybe it is an apocryphal story.

Camille Brenner did not go broke but became a millionaire and built a new hotel which he called the Parkhotel. It opened in 1914, a few months before World War I. Many hotels have had their troubles since then but Brenner's Parkhotel, which includes part of the Stephanie, is now synonymous with Baden-Baden. Americans especially talk of 'Brenner's' when they mean Baden-Baden. It remains one of the last truly great hotels in Europe. Progress has been introduced in a subtle way, so that one does not notice it. A card in the room tells you the first name of your maid and your valet. There is loving attention to every detail: flowers, linen, silver, breakfast, food. A few years ago, they had more employees than beds. One of them is Walter Putz. His passion is for perfect dining-room service, his hobby collecting very old cook books. His private collection of over a thousand books, begins with Platina, *De Honesta Voluptate*, published 1475 in Piadeno, Italy, and includes rare editions of great cookery books during the last five centuries.

Prior to the last war, Brenner's Parkhotel would close in winter and the staff would spend the cold season in the palatial hotels of Egypt and the Riviera. Now the Park stays open all year to keep its impeccably trained staff. The employees respect the guests' strangest whims. Service of pronounced individuality is a 'must'. Your likes and dislikes are noted in personal files. Whenever you return, they will try to give you the same or a similar room, the extra-hard pillow you requested on your last visit, and your writing table will be placed exactly where you wanted it then. The clientèle is truly international, from Victorian ladies with Victorian dogs to German industrialists. For a long time Americans led the international guest list but that has changed. To get a room during the season, especially during the 'great week' late in August you must be a guest of long standing. Newcomers have little chance of getting in between April and October. After four weeks even 'old' guests are politely but firmly asked to leave. 'Sorry, that's a house rule.' The reception clerks are masters of the vague apology and the diplomatic turndown.

Of course there are other good hotels, and some were run for generations as patriarchal institutions. One of the oldest, Bad-Hotel zum Hirsch, has been in the same family for five hundred years. I once stayed at the Bellevue, owned by the Saur family. Their ancestors were executioners and surgeons and eventually bought a modest forty-room hotel which they gradually expanded into a beautifully furnished manor house with 145 rooms and five acres of beautiful grounds. The ancestors were avid collectors and there are equestrian drawings, paintings and old furniture everywhere and the place looks more like an elegantly decorated home than a palatial hotel. Once upon a time, there was a hydraulic lift that was serviced by a youngster. He got bed, meals and tips. Now there are automatic elevators, and for how long will there be a *liftier* telling people to watch their step please? Still, hotel owners in Baden-Baden are more fortunate than elsewhere. The place will always attract people, it offers so many things to so many people. Modern people stay at the Europäischer Hof that belongs to the Steigenberger chain, possibly the Hiltons of Germany. There are hotels in the middle of the golf course, in the forests, in the old town, out of town. In Baden-Baden the choice of a hotel is a matter of one's pocket book and personal philosophy.

To the nostalgic the spa offers a sense of the past, which is adroitly and successfully kept up, and a feeling of inner relaxation. It is enhanced by the silhouette of the hills, the familiar face of the old concierge, and the spa orchestra that performs from Easter to the end of September three times a day at the Kurhaus or in the gardens, weather permitting. They play the same atrocious arrangement of Schubert's 'Unfinished Symphony' that

Two mid nineteenth-century lithographs after drawings by Jacottet.

below People conversing outside the Kurhaus.

right The ruins of an old castle buried in the hills of the Black Forest, a popular sight-seeing spot for visitors to Baden-Baden.

their predecessors played half a century ago. Nowadays there are also symphony concerts under well-known conductors, organ recitals at the Stiftskirche and evening serenades at Schloss Favourite and the New Schloss. There are theatrical performances, private art galleries and a State Art Gallery. Other people come to fish and hunt, to play tennis, to ride, to swim at the Schwarzwald Schwimmstadion, to take lessons in flying planes and helicopters, to go rock climbing on the Battert by the Old Schloss, to shoot at the rifle range of the Eichenwald Schützenverein, to take part in the ballroom dancing competitions every Friday at the Kurhaus.

Above all, there are beautiful excursions into the Black Forest, a wooded paradise with dreamy moorland tarns, lush carpets of dark-green moss, fir-scented paths. One is called 'philosophers' path', as in Heidelberg, to remind you that you are in the land of poets and thinkers. The soporific sounds of waterfalls are wonderfully relaxing. It is twenty minutes by car to Bühlerhöhe, where Konrad Adenauer used to spend his summers, a gloomy structure with a dark courtyard reminiscent of the prison scene in Beethoven's 'Fidelio'. The place was given by an adoring woman to Kaiser Wilhelm II. He sent her a thank-you note and then turned it over to his officers, who were not delighted.

The Black Forest Hochstrasse is a beautiful highway leading along the crest of the wooded mountains to the resort of Freudenstadt, 'City of Joys'. There are tempting inns where the smell of mushrooms fried in butter drifts out from the kitchen. And there are small wine-producing villages along the Badische Weinstrasse (Baden Wine Road) that was created in 1954 and starts in Baden-Baden. There is also the Ortenauer Weinpfad for pedestrians who like to explore in a leisurely way the wine-growing region from Baden-Baden to Offenburg. There are vineyards in the vicinity producing quality wines. In Neuweier, Varnhalt and Steinbach-Umweg the wines come in *Bocksbeutel*, the flat, big-bellied bottles which are reserved for Franconian wines. The Schloss vineyards of Neuweier have enjoyed this privilege for a hundred and fifty years.

It is a pleasant, rich part of the country where the slow-spoken people work hard but take their time over substantial meals. They prefer quantity to quality. They like to eat five meals a day, with snacks and drinks – heavy white wine – in between. 'A goose is a silly fowl,' they say, 'too large for one person, too small for two.'

But when all is said and done, people go to Baden-Baden for two reasons: to gamble and to take the cure. The Germans are serious, often solemn gamblers. The night I was at the Casino, many were working hard with pencils and statistics, studying mathematical combinations, and then they lost. There were also the inevitable tourists with the greedy gleam in their eyes, trying to make a quick fortune, hoping to break the bank. In the

Salon Pompadour people were gambling with solid gold chips which were coined for the Casino by special permission of the Federal Republic's Finance Ministry. The Ministry always wins at the Casino, raking in eighty per cent of the house profits.

I remember a dour-looking man with heavy eyebrows, who lost a lot of money and looked very tense. He was obviously suffering from stress and I wondered why they let him gamble but perhaps he was on Anti-Stress II, without medical supervision. I was wrong. I met him again the next morning at the Friedrichsbad. He told me he had been sent there by his *Kurarzt* 'to relax and renew my zest for living'.

An elderly attendant with the dignified bearing of a German university professor received me and helped me to undress. He weighed me and then directed me through a full-course menu of hydrotherapy. I was ordered to shower, then sent to a dry hot-air (102 degrees) room, massaged and rubbed down, sent to a steam bath, and again to a cold shower. I no longer had any zest for living. For over an hour, I jumped from hot water into cold thermal baths and back into hot, showered again, was told to drink healing waters, went into effervescent baths, and began jumping from hot into cold into hot. There is something sad and touching about a group of naked, middle-aged and elderly men jumping in and out of hot and cold baths, hoping to emerge feeling a little less old.

The dour-looking man who had gambled and lost the night before told me he came here three times a week.

'Only place in this damn town where I am able to relax', he said. 'Yesterday black came out 209 times on table number one. Red came out 166 times. You wouldn't believe it. I was betting on red.'

I nodded sympathetically. He sighed deeply and jumped into the cold water. I jumped into the hot.

At the end of the ordeal I was welcomed back into the dry world by my professor-attendant, packed into warm blankets, carefully placed on an inner spring mattress and told to relax. When I awoke an hour later I was weighed again. I had lost two pounds. As I left, the professor invited me to come back again and try some of the other attractions: the oxygen baths, thermal foam baths, mud packs, whole electric-air baths, damp inhalation, artificial sunlight treatment, thermal effervescent air baths and medical vaporization (whatever that is).

Maybe I will come back to Baden-Baden some day. Not so much to renew my zest for living or to gamble, but because it is such a beautiful place.

Bad Homburg

A detail from a view of Bad Homburg
and the Taunus hills behind.

In the English-speaking world a Homburg is an elegant hat but in Germany Bad Homburg is a spa. The Homburg hat was of course born in Bad Homburg. The Prince of Wales, later Edward VII, whose historical achievements are prominent in the world of fashion and trend-setting, liked the hats of the local militiamen and later wore the fancy adaptation known as the Homburg. It is still the favourite head-gear of diplomats and other people who wish to look dignified. According to tradition, it was in Bad Homburg that the Prince once forgot to fasten the lower button on his waistcoat. Ever since men, not only diplomats, wearing a waistcoat leave the lowest waistcoat button unbuttoned. Male fashions may fade away but never die.

Bad Homburg – its complete name is Bad Homburg vor der Höhe – is much older than the hat. Its mineral springs had been known for centuries and the location at the foot of the Taunus hills, 'vor der Höhe', made it a favourite excursion for the people in Frankfurt am Main, only ten miles away. Not every city has a suburb such as Bad Homburg. No wonder that the most famous family in Frankfurt, the Rothschilds, soon owned most of the small Principality of Homburg. (I am well aware that the most famous individual in Frankfurt remains Johann Wolfgang Goethe, born there in 1749.)

Homburg's great history began later, in 1840, when the great entrepreneur François Blanc showed up there. Blanc is the man who later set up the most famous casino of all, in Monte Carlo, but that was after 1866 when Prussia annexed Homburg and ordered the Homburg Casino closed. The Homburgers naturally take a patronizing attitude toward Monte Carlo. Blanc did for Homburg what the Bénazets, at about the same time, did for Baden-Baden. It is not wise to mention Baden-Baden in Bad Homburg, or vice versa.

Blanc had the ruling Prince sign a few contracts and went to work. He extended the spa park and developed the old mineral springs. The friends of Bad Homburg, of whom there are many in Germany, call the *Kurpark* the country's most beautiful. You are beginning to understand why it is not wise to make comparisons with Baden-Baden which is so proud of the Lichtentaler Allee. No doubt the *Kurpark* of Bad Homburg is a magnificent monument to nineteenth-century art-of-living. Lawns and brooks and ponds and water lilies and pergolas. A Siamese temple in gold and crimson that was built by King Chulalongkorn, a faithful Homburg *Kurgast*, and renovated in 1960 by the present King of Thailand who also likes Homburg. The onion-towered Russian chapel which Tsar Nicholas II inaugurated in 1899. Some Russian monarchists – there still exist a few of them, though they are very old – go there to pray. The small casino is there which François Blanc set up when he came to Homburg. Tennis

The elegant Kurhaus and gardens where emperors, kings, and statesmen from all over the world were entertained.

courts and golf links and the famous Tennis Bar, off the courts. And nowadays the elegant bungalows built along the rim of the *Kurpark* by rich people who make their money in Frankfurt, the country's big commercial and banking centre. Frankfurt is not a beautiful city and it is pleasant to drive to Bad Homburg in the late afternoon and spend the weekend there.

François Blanc did not foresee this late development but otherwise he showed great prophetic genius. His *Kurhaus* was a marvel of contemporary elegance. He understood that it is not enough for a spa to have warm springs and spa doctors. He knew the almost mystical relation between sinning and gambling. He brought great artists to Bad Homburg who became the talk of Europe. Adelina Patti was paid five thousand gulden for a night's performance at the Kurhaus-Casino, and Blanc did not mind because Patti immediately gambled and lost all the money and more at the Casino.

Blanc knew that any spa is only as good as its celebrities; the theory is still valid today when you read about modern celebrities going to Marbella, St Tropez, Acapulco. M. Blanc did not bother with stars and starlets; they did not exist then anyway. He brought emperors, kings and statesmen to Bad Homburg. Gladstone came from England, Garibaldi came from Italy, and Prince Lucien Bonaparte, a nephew of the Emperor, not only came but broke the bank in 1852. Thereupon many members of French society arrived perhaps in order to break the bank, but many left broke. A song which was popular ended with the words, '*C'est toujours Blanc qui gagne.*' Not red and not black, but white would win in the end.

Between 1870 and 1914, Bad Homburg had a very aristocratic *cachet*. Kaiser Wilhelm I of Germany showed up in May and then again in August. Since he also went to other spas mentioned in this book, it is hard to understand how he found time to rule Germany between visits. In Bad Homburg the Kaiser conducted his imperial manoeuvres, his great car races, and it was there that his grandson, Kaiser Wilhelm II commanded a parade of Zeppelins. His Majesty also inspected the reconstruction of the nearby Saalburg, an ancient Roman castellum which is now popular with sightseers. The younger Wilhelm is said to have marched through the *Kurpark* – he marched, he would not just walk – and to have snapped his fingers at trees which he did not like. The trees had to be felled. He also stamped his foot and pointed at a spot, and there a new tree had to be planted. There are still people in Bad Homburg who swear it happened that way.

The other celebrated visitor was the Prince of Wales who had his own massage room in the *Kurhaus* and was very serious about the cure. It is hard to believe that he lost some forty pounds every summer there, at any rate he soon went back to Maxim's and regained his weight. He arrived with a retinue of gentlemen-in-waiting who were said to breakfast with champagne at the Café Brahe (now known as the Café Schmidt), and ended their day with a champagne supper at the Casino restaurant. All kinds of stories are told about the visitors from Britain. Did they really load pretty young ladies into wheelbarrows and race them through the woods? Anyway they had fun and properly shocked the elderly ladies from England and Germany who came to Homburg to 'take the waters'.

Blanc was gone by that time but 'his' spa remained famous. The Kings of Siam (as noted), Sweden, Greece came there, the ruler of Bulgaria, the Tsar of Russia, Bismark and Hindenburg, maharajas from India and millionaires. The clientèle seems to be the same in all great spas but after all these were the people who could afford them. The Krupps and Opels from Germany, the Goulds and Harrimans from America. Countess Sophia Kisselev was carried to the roulette table every afternoon; she was said to gamble from 2 p.m. to 2 a.m. It was rumoured that she did not mind losing because she owned shares of the Casino, and the bets she lost came back as dividends. Such stories help a gambling place.

One happily remembers a Polish nobleman, Baron von Kosten-Gantzkow, who arrived in an elegant coach drawn by four horses, and in no time lost the coach, the horses, his estates, and even his silk jackets. Prince Proworoff, the Tsar's state-secretary, was popular because he appeared every morning on the promenade with two dozen roses and gave them away to the beautiful ladies he met. The story does not say whether they went there to meet the *Rosenonkel*, as they called him.

It is impossible to invent such stories. They must have happened. One only reports them. They are the fairy-tale stuff of which the pre-war dream spas were made. It was a world that could not last and it did not. Some spas perished then and some survived. Bad Homburg survived, but for a while it had to change.

Edward VII used to stay at Bad Homburg to take the cure and lost as much as 40 lbs on every visit. Here, wearing a Homburg hat, he is surrounded by members of the English court, on a picnic at Herschgarten near Bad Homburg.

At the end of the First World War, the rich were no longer rich. Bad Homburg became a spa for National Health people who needed the medicinal waters. Suddenly, the sort of people went there who could never afford it in the old days. There was much indignation among the old Homburgers, and the older gentlemen of the spa management thought it was awful. But it was not awful. The National Health patients saved the spa at a time when many others disappeared. The old ladies still came, not so rich, and they complained about these 'new' people who now showed up at the *Wandelhalle*, the Promenade Hall, to drink the waters.

The finest hotel in town is Ritter's Parkhotel. It now belongs to the Steigenberger chain. During the Nazi era, now only dimly remembered, the SS had one of its *Lebensborn* ('life fountain') establishments there. Beautiful specimens of Aryan womenhood were encouraged to sleep with elite members of the SS, blond and blue-eyed, to give birth to one-hundred-per-cent pure Aryans. The plan misfired, and the Aryan establishments vanished in 1945, when the sturdy Americans appeared.

But Bad Homburg was lucky. During a few months, General Eisenhower, then the commander of the Allied forces in Germany, lived in the Haus-im-Wald, at the rim of the Kurpark. He said it was beautiful and he slept there so well. No wonder, others have felt like that before. But General Eisenhower set a trend, and after John McCloy, the American High Commissioner, lived in Bad Homburg for some time, the trend became an avalanche. Suddenly, everybody remembered that Bad Homburg had always been beautiful, and that one should go there. And everybody went. If you talk to a spa doctor privately, he may admit that the cure is too difficult for someone who is really sick, and not effective for someone who is healthy, but that it may help the many people in between who are neither healthy nor really sick.

Everything is well organized in Bad Homburg, from the *Kurkarte*, spa membership card, that tells the cure guest exactly which waters to sip and how much and how, 'One drinks with small swallows . . . walking slowly up and down', to the exact instructions given by your doctor. American doctors often consider the instructions silly. German patients think they are holy. And since the first prerequisite of a cure is to believe in it, the patients who believe in their doctors will perhaps become healthy in Bad Homburg.

Today there are three different groups of people in the once famous spa that is again quite fashionable. There are still the private cure-takers, dignified members of the middle classes, who go to Homburg because it is 'wonderful'. Second, there are the National Health people who are sent there and take the cure, because it costs them nothing. And third, there are the rich people from Frankfurt, who live there in their fine, new houses.

The three groups do not mix. It is even doubtful that any of them know of the existence of the others. It is still a serious business in Germany to go to a spa like Bad Homburg. They think that your life may depend on it. But Homburg is no longer a full-time spa. It is also a town with 56,000 inhabitants, with cafeterias, modern stores, high buildings, and terrific traffic jams. The lovely old Schloss is still there, and it is being photographed, but if you want to be in the *old* Bad Homburg, you have to go out to the *Kurpark* where (almost) nothing has changed. And if you close your eyes and think hard, you may find yourself in the never-never world of the past when Bad Homburg was a spa and not the name of a hat.

The Landgrafenschloss and gardens showing the thirteenth-century white tower of the old Ritterburg.

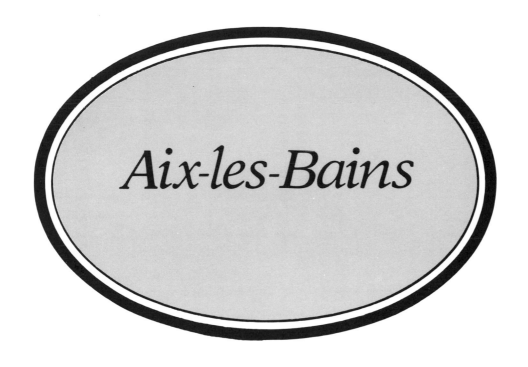

The main square of Aix-les-Bains.

Aix-les-Bains in Savoy, not to be confused with Aix-en-Provence, is another fascinating example of a once great spa that has since made a spectacular comeback. The great time in Aix-les-Bains was the Belle Epoque when the lovely spa, located half-way between Geneva and Lyon, attracted kings and queens and, naturally, their ambitious subjects. Between 1885 and 1890, Queen Victoria went there three times and even had an elegant villa built, right next to the Villa des Fleurs which was then a gambling casino. Not exactly a Victorian location. Of course, the Queen would not gamble. That would be too much. Maybe she liked to know who was going to the casino.

Around 1890, Aix-les-Bains was perhaps the most elegant spa on earth. Dom Pedro II, the Emperor of Brazil, went there, and so did the Empress Elisabeth of Austria, who always went where the action was, Maria Pia Queen Mother of Portugal, Queen Emma and later Queen Wilhelmine of Holland, Leopold II King of the Belgians, and George I King of Greece. Each ruler had his official court, and each court was followed by the inevitable hangers-on. Dignitaries, ministers, ambassadors. In those years Aix had a unique role in the life of international society. 'Aix' was of course synonymous with Aix-les-Bains. No one had ever heard of the other Aix, down in Provence, which now has a university and even a festival of its own.

True, Aix-les-Bains had hot springs, and the doctors proclaimed that the waters were good for arthritis and many other ills but 'for many visitors the cure was only a pretext'. It was not for Paul Verlaine, the great French poet who came there in 1899 to cure his arthritis. Verlaine had no money but he wrote later of Doctor Guilland, Doctor Cazalis and Doctor Monard who were extremely 'generous'; they probably sent him no bills. And the chef de police was 'charming and saw at once that I wasn't a robber though I certainly looked like one'. Later Verlaine wrote about the cure, 'You undress and enter the pool, and later two characters turn jets of water against you. The water is hot, slightly sulphurous and unpleasant. You are being massaged which is almost voluptuous. Then you stand up and they turn the water against you again. The water is strong and you would fall down if you weren't standing next to a wall. Afterwards one rests or tries to sleep. That is all I do here . . .'

Aix-les-Bains is very old. It was perhaps founded in the first century AD, and was then known as Aquae Allobrogum. It is very proud of two Roman ruins. The Arch of Campanus is absolutely genuine. Pompeius Campanus was a rich Roman who wanted to secure his immortality, locally anyway. In this he succeeded. There are some doubts among the experts about the so-called Temple of Diana that may have been built later; there is a charming vagueness about the beginnings of the place. Julius Caesar stopped here when he came to conquer the Gauls, and liked it very much, and after

A spa patient in a sedan chair outside the baths in the 1940s. Spa visitors to Aix-les-Bains were transported from their hotels to the baths in these covered chairs.

him the rich and powerful Romans came there and enjoyed the hot springs. We know already that the Romans were great believers in hot waters.

Then nothing seems to have happened for a while. The writer and historian Baccius claims that Charles the Great ordered the restoration of the hot springs of Aix-en-Savoie, as it was then called. Today many historians admit that this is 'difficult to prove'. But a great expert, the Comte de Loche, writes that Baccius, who was secretary and physician of Pope Sixtus v, was 'very conscientious' and why would he make such a statement if it was not true? Charlemagne loved the hot springs – they were restored all over Europe – and that he was in Savoy is proved in the *Chanson de Roland*.

The Middle Ages remain dark and undocumented in the spa. We know that Rudolph iii of Burgundy on 24 April 1011 gave the place to his second wife Ermengarde. The memorable document exists and 'almost' coincides with the foundation of Rome, they claim in Aix. The place was then part of the Duchy of Burgundy. In the twelfth and thirteenth centuries, Gauthier d'Aix, Rodolphe d'Aix and Humbert de Seyssel are mentioned among the seigneurs of Aix. Henri iv appeared with the beautiful Henriette d'Entragues and appreciated the thermal springs 'with much pleasure and contentment'. Apparently the success of Aix was assured and many famous people came for the cure, among them the Duc de Lesdiguières and the Duchesse Hortense Mancini. In 1776, King Victor Amadeus III had the first thermal establishment built. At the end of the century they already had forty houses '*pour recevoir les étrangers*'. A certain Cabias was quoted for having praised 'the wonderful virtues of baths of Aix-en-Savoie'. Doctor Jean Pauchoud, physician of the king, told his patients to go to Aix and drink six cups of the good water every day. It is reported that there were 760 visitors in 1791, but many of them did not come for the cure, they wanted to get away from Paris where life was getting pretty hectic, especially after the massacre of the Champs de Mars. The following year, only 332 visitors came to Aix. In Paris, three men – Marat, Danton and Robespierre – became leaders of public opinion.

On 22 September 1792, the French general Montesquieu gave his troops orders to march into Savoy. The invasion was peaceful, members of the nobility went to Spain and elsewhere, and the local writer Joseph de Maistre declared that the French Revolution 'represented a great epoch in human history, whether one likes it or not'. In July, 1793, the Councillors of Aix voted in favour of the human rights of all citizens and adopted the Constitution written by the National Convention. 'By its courageous stand the municipality of Aix-en-Savoie placed itself at the avant-garde of an irresistible movement', writes Henry Planche. Did Queen Victoria and the other Majesties know the revolutionary background of the elegant spa, when they went there a century later?

But a few things happened in between. Several members of Napoleon's family discovered Aix. The emperor never went there, but his sister Pauline, the handsome widow of General Leclerc, came to Aix and stayed at the elegant Villa Chevalley which still exists. Pauline married a Borghese Prince and Napoleon made him governor of the departments 'd'au delà des Alpes', with an official residence in Turin, but it was no secret that after 1808 Pauline stayed in Aix and began to play the part of the governor's wife. Prince Borghese wisely stayed in Turin and Pauline pretended to be sick and said she had to take the cure in Aix where everybody knew that the cure was named Monsieur Forbin, Pauline's new lover. When the Bonaparte family found out about this escapade, Queen Mother Loetitia and Pauline's uncle, Cardinal Fesch, went to Aix where Pauline admitted that she was in fine health and gave up Monsieur Forbin. The following year she went to another Aix, this time Aix-la-Chapelle (now Aachen in Germany) and tried the waters there and promptly took another lover.

But in France Aix-en-Savoie and the Villa Chevalley had become famous and it was no accident that Joséphine came there, after her husband, the emperor, had thrown her out. Joséphine was accompanied by a Madame de Remusat, but though both were incognito, everybody in Aix knew their

Robert Lefèvre's portrait of Pauline Bonaparte, Emperor Napoleon I's sister, who stayed at the Villa Chevalley in Aix-les-Bains and while there became involved in a scandalous love affair.

true identities. She was later joined by her daughter Hortense, who had left her husband Louis Bonaparte, King of Holland. Hortense lived in a smaller house outside the town with her two sons, one of whom was later Napoleon III, but she often visited her mother at the Villa Chevalley. It was soon noticed that a certain Charles de Flahaut was often present and became what was known in Aix as Hortense's *consolateur attentionné*, 'the attentive consoler'. The French always have a word for it. Everybody was scandalized and many people went to Aix to watch the goings-on. It was wonderful publicity when Joséphine, returning from an outing to the Abbey de Hautecombe, was almost drowned, and was saved by Flahaut, naturally.

The following year Hortense returned to Aix alone and when she left she got lost between Geneva and Paris. The mystery is now explained in the memoirs of Marie-Louise Pailleron which were published in 1935 after a decent interval. Hortense had stopped near Chambéry at the estate of

An old drawing of the 'Cascade de Grésy'. The village of Grésy lies just outside Aix-les-Bains.

the eminent physician, Aimé Rey, and there gave birth to a healthy boy who later became the influential half-brother of Napoleon III, and remains known as the Duc de Morny.

Among all the spas of Europe, Aix-les-Bains has the most interesting 'chronique scandaleuse', no doubt about that. There was a particularly brilliant season in 1812, when Pauline re-appeared, always beautiful, now under the name of Duchess de Guastalla. Many other beautiful women appeared – Queen Caroline, the wife of Murat, and Julie Clary, the wife of the King of Spain. It is hard to keep up with the complications of the Almanac de Gotha in these turbulent years. Most interesting of all was the Duchesse d'Abrantes, whose love affairs while in Aix scandalized and delighted everybody. Pauline lived in an elegant house in the Rue des Soupirs, 'Street of Sighs', known after the sighs of all the lovers she had there, among them the great actor Talma. Alas, in 1855 the municipality changed the name of the Street of Sighs to the Avenue Victoria, in honour of the

Le Grand Cercle, a gambling casino, which was opened in 1849 with Victor Emmanuel II as guest of honour.

English sovereign. There are now people in Aix who prefer the old name. But the memory of 1812 is unforgotten. While Pauline carried on, Loetitia came back with her brother, Cardinal Fesch, and Joséphine made a reappearance, and also Hortense. And to make matters even more interesting, Marie-Louise, the second wife of Napoleon Bonaparte, came in 1815 while her husband was on the island of Elba. According to local chroniclers she met there the Count Neipperg who became her great and intimate friend. The affair which later scandalized the courts of Europe began in Aix. Ever since, members of the family Bonaparte have come back to the charming spa. In 1969, a young Prince Bonaparte went to school at the Lyçée Bertholet in Annecy. Everybody in Aix-les-Bains was very pleased.

No one has been able to explain the great attraction of Aix-les-Bains. It may be the pleasant climate, the nearness of the Lac du Bourget, the location between Geneva and Lyon, the proximity of the mountains. The poet Alphonse de Lamartine came there for the cure, stayed at the house of Doctor Perrier (it no longer exists) and under the spell of Aix promptly fell in love with a Madame Charles. He has written about it in his novel *Raphaël*. Julie Charles soon died, but the poet, with customary license, met Marie-Antoinette Bancel and after a while Lena de Larche. And after Lamartine, Aix was established as a 'romantic' spa. Madame de Staël came there and soon found herself in the arms of Benjamin Constant. Balzac wrote about Aix; George Sand made an appearance, smoked cigars, and carried on; Stendhal and Alexandre Dumas wrote about the happenings of Aix.

But the glory of Aix had only begun. On 15 July 1849, the Grand Cercle was opened, as a gambling casino, and Victor Emmanuel II and his wife were the guests of honour. In the great auditorium of the Grand Cercle, an ambitious opera company performed Wagner's *Tristan und Isolde* and later Saint-Saëns' *Samson et Dalila*. Savoy had become French and Napoleon III and the Empress Eugénie came to Aix and were received by the municipality. Emperor Napoleon III reminisced about his youth in Aix and about his mother, Queen Hortense, who had lived there. Ten years later, Napoleon III was finished, and the municipality sent a telegram to Gambetta, 'The Republic was called out here in Aix yesterday evening at ten o'clock.' Very soon President Sadi Carnot came to Aix and was officially received there, perhaps by some of the same officials who had ten years ago bowed deeply to the Emperor.

This lack of character did not keep Queen Victoria from coming to Aix-les-Bains which became a social must for English society. It seems that Princess Beatrice had come alone to Aix in 1883 to take the treatment under Docteur Francis Bertier. When she returned to London, she spoke so highly of Aix that her mother came there in April 1885, under the name of the

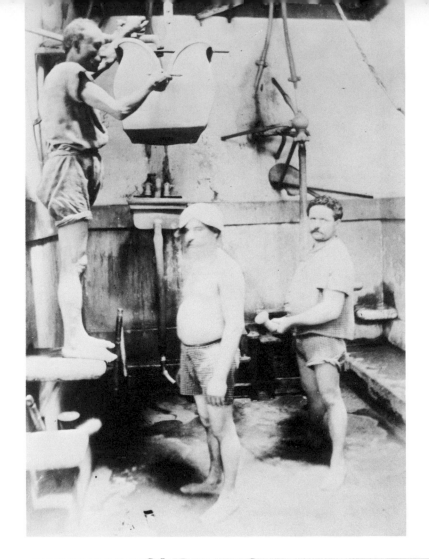

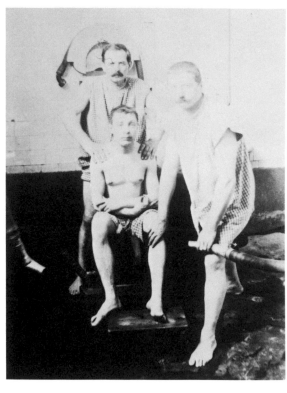

Spa guests undergoing different treatments at the baths at Aix in the 1940s. The hot sulphurous waters are particularly recommended for oto-rhino-laryngological ailments.

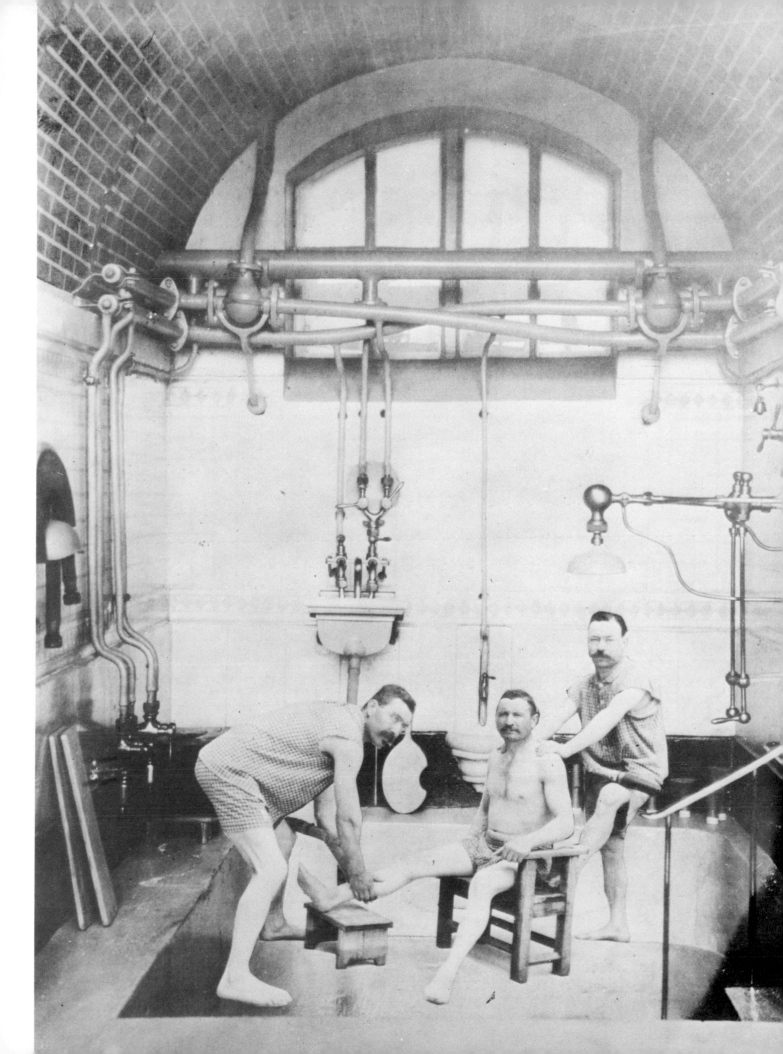

Countess of Balmoral. Nobody was deceived about the incognito, and the populace came to pay its reverence. Princess Beatrice was there, and among the entourage was also a Lady Churchill. Queen Victoria liked it so much that she returned for two other visits, in 1887 and 1890. After that, the prestige of Aix-les-Bains was made. During the season of 1908, for instance, the King of Greece came there, the Queen of Italy, Sarah Bernhardt, and 'several hundred' famous people from France, Russia, the United States, Rumania and Greece. But above all, there were the English. A visit to Aix in the years prior to the First World War was almost obligatory.

After 1914, Aix-les-Bains had the same problems as the other playgrounds of once-famous people. During the Belle Epoque some of the finest hotels in Europe had been constructed in the elegant spa. There exists a collection of postcards, published as a small book, that show the glory of Aix prior to 1914. The Palace Hotel Regina Bernascon, the Villa Regina, the Hotel Beau-Site, the Hotel d'Albion, the Hotel Excelsior, the Hotel Splendide, and the Hotel Royal (which was opened in 1914 and became a hospital). Some of these great hotels, like the Regina Bernascon, have become public monuments, and cannot have their façades changed. It has been subdivided into apartments. The same fate has happened to the Splendide, the Royal, the Excelsior, the Mirabeau. All hotels had their spacious private parks.

After the Second Warld War, the municipality of Aix-les-Bains had to make some hard decisions. The great past was gone, one had to think of the future. Aix still has the Villa Chevalley once inhabited by Josephine, and the former Grand Cercle, now known as Palais de Savoie. But the modern spa also has a small airport Aix-Chambéry, a racecourse, and the Grand Port. On the Lac du Bourget there are regattas. Along the lake there are camping sites. The future of the city (which now has 30,000 inhabitants) depends on three sources of income: the hot springs that are still there, tourism, and industry. The cure can now be taken in ultramodern establishments in Aix and Marlioz. Kings and queens no longer go there but people who need the treatment do. In 1951, there were 14,600 patients. Last year, there were over 45,000. The waters of Aix are particularly recommended to people suffering from oto-rhino-laryngological ailments.

Much attracts the tourists, from the beautiful plage to the surrounding mountains. Industry keeps to the southern side of the town, so that it will not mingle with tourists and health seekers. Aix-les-Bains has discovered the pleasures of gastronomy. From the Lac du Bourget comes the delicate *omble chevalier* (char), one of the finest fishes on earth. It can be fished only during a short season, at dawn, in very cold water, and is highly appreciated in the temples of gastronomy. The famous restaurant Pyramide in Vienne,

The baths and main hotels at Aix-les-Bains. The Roman Arch of Campanus is in the foreground.

Isère, receives its seasonal supply of *omble chevalier* from the Lac du Bourget. Savoy is also famous for its cheeses; the great Reblochon and the famous Beaufort come from the region, also the Tomme de Savoie and the Vacherin.

Aix-les-Bains now offers a fine selection of Roman ruins, modern thermal establishments, a gambling casino, the remarkable Musée Fauré, great parks, the lake with its attractions, and an almost ideal location on the superhighway that will soon be finished from Geneva to Lyon. There will be a Chamber Music Festival, and there is already an International Dance Festival. It cannot have been easy to forget the glorious past and plan for the future but the Aixois (as the local people call themselves) have done it. In the sixteenth century the poet Jacques Pelletier wrote a poem, '*Nous reviendrons à Aix*' (We shall come back to Aix). This has become the semi-official motto of the inhabitants. They hope that everybody will come back to Aix-les-Bains.

The lake of Bourget, on which the town
Aix-les-Bains borders; the Great Rock of
the Chambotte is to the left.

The Spas of Eugénie

An early pen and wash of the coast
around Biarritz by the French painter,
Garneray.

The borderline between a health spa and a mere resort is flexible. Nowadays people are becoming health-conscious, and it is relatively easy to install some kind of treatment. But a self-respecting spa, in order to be rediscovered today, must have a glamorous past and possibly royalty in its history. What Empress Elisabeth of Habsburg was to Ischl and Meran, Edward VII to Baden-Baden and Bad Homburg, the Empress Eugénie, wife of Napoleon III, was to Biarritz and Eugénie-les-Bains.

Eugénie de Montijo, a pretty girl from a rich Spanish family, lived in Paris at 12, Place Vendôme – the very house where Chopin died on 17 October 1849, at the age of thirty-nine. At a reception held in the house, Napoleon III met Eugénie and later married her. Eugénie liked to spend the summers in the south-western corner of France not far from Spain. In 1854 she and Napoleon III made their summer home in the small fishing village of Biarritz which was then an unspoiled place and must have been lovely. The court came there, and in due time there were the aristocrats and the rich people trying to be like the aristocrats. Their Majesties had a luxurious villa built, or rather a uper villa which has become the Palais at 1, Avenue Impératrice. It has been modernized and has an ocean-front swimming pool which was not there at the time of Empress Eugénie. Prior to World II Biarritz was truly a royal retreat where the high and mighty met. It was a favourite place for kings who went there anonymously.

above An engraving of Eugénie, the beautiful Spanish girl who married the Emperor Napoleon III and gave her name to the spas of this region.

below Villa Eugénie, the palatial summer residence of the Emperor Napoleon III and Empress Eugénie at Biarritz during the 1860s.

St-Jean-de-Luz. An old fishing village, now a popular resort, on the French Basque coast where Louis XIV and Marie Thérèse of Spain were married. After the marriage ceremony they returned to the Maison de l'Infante, shown here, to throw specially struck coins to the crowds outside.

During the war few people went to Biarritz but in the 1950s the place had an astonishing revival, and it is now considered superior to the Riviera or Deauville. It has two casinos, the Municipal and the Bellevue, and it has great hotels, above all Le Palais, *the* great palace in the southwest of France 'which maintains the traditions of an *époque de grand luxe*'. It has the Atlantic Ocean and a beautiful beach and is said to be the surfing capital of Europe.

Best of all, Biarritz has a very picturesque neighbourhood, and there are people who like the neighbourhood better than even Biarritz. In Biarritz you can spend the morning on the beach, bathing and surfing, and lunch in a mountain resort. Bayonne, with its bullfights and Léon Bonnat museum, its cathedral and old ramparts is a few miles away. Nearby is Saint-Jean-de-Luz, an old fishing village where Louis XIV married Marie Thérèse of Spain. And there is Hendaye, at the Spanish border, with its beautiful beach. The old port of Biarritz, Le Vieux Port, reminds us of the whaling days of the erstwhile village.

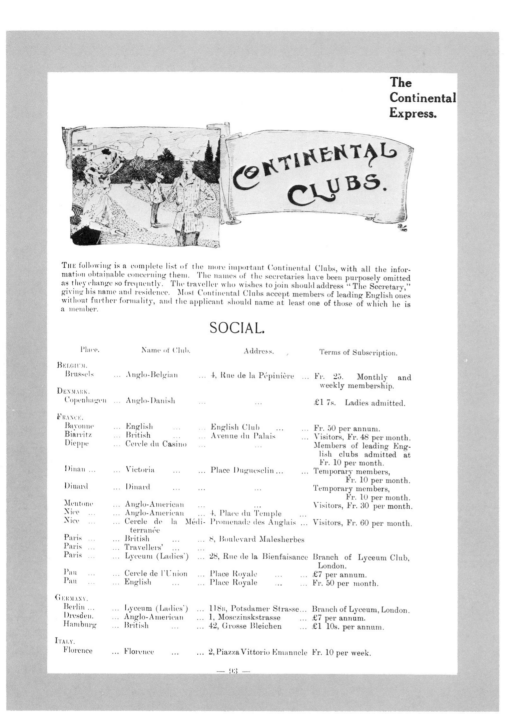

CONTINENTAL CLUBS.

THE following is a complete list of the more important Continental Clubs, with all the information obtainable concerning them. The names of the secretaries have been purposely omitted as they change so frequently. The traveller who wishes to join should address "The Secretary," giving his name and residence. Most Continental Clubs accept members of leading English ones without further formality, and the applicant should name at least one of those of which he is a member.

SOCIAL.

Place.	Name of Club.	Address.	Terms of Subscription.
BELGIUM.			
Brussels	Anglo-Belgian	4, Rue de la Pépinière	Fr. 25. Monthly and weekly membership.
DENMARK.			
Copenhagen	Anglo-Danish		£1 7s. Ladies admitted.
FRANCE.			
Bayonne	English	English Club	Fr. 50 per annum.
Biarritz	British	Avenue du Palais	Visitors, Fr. 48 per month.
Dieppe	Cercle du Casino		Members of leading English clubs admitted at Fr. 10 per month.
Dinan	Victoria	Place Duguesclin	Temporary members, Fr. 10 per month.
Dinard	Dinard		Temporary members, Fr. 10 per month.
Mentone	Anglo-American		Visitors, Fr. 30 per month.
Nice	Anglo-American	4, Place du Temple	
Nice	Cercle de la Méditerranée	Promenade des Anglais	Visitors, Fr. 60 per month.
Paris	British	8, Boulevard Malesherbes	
Paris	Travellers'		
Paris	Lyceum (Ladies')	28, Rue de la Bienfaisance	Branch of Lyceum Club, London.
Pau	Cercle de l'Union	Place Royale	£7 per annum.
Pau	English	Place Royale	Fr. 50 per month.
GERMANY.			
Berlin	Lyceum (Ladies')	118B, Potsdamer Strasse	Branch of Lyceum, London.
Dresden	Anglo-American	1, Mosczinskstrasse	£7 per annum.
Hamburg	British	42, Grosse Bleichen	£1 10s. per annum.
ITALY.			
Florence	Florence	2, Piazza Vittorio Emanuele	Fr. 10 per week.

— 93 —

A page from the magazine *Continental Express Illustrated*, 1909, showing the fashionable clubs at which to stay when visiting the Continent.

It seems that Biarritz defies change. Gone are the days when Queen Victoria came here and was Napoleon's guest; when her son, Edward VII, held his summer court here every year from 1906 to 1910; when the Duke and the Duchess of Windsor arrived on the overnight from Paris. July is crowded and in August it is almost impossible to get a room in a hotel. In September there are art exhibitions for the wealthy and trotting races. The Hotel du Palais is truly an old-fashioned gala place. It has marble bathrooms that are almost as large as the rooms; you will be shown the one Winston Churchill used. There is a profusion of red plush and gold velvet. For people who like an elegant vacation even in our inelegant age, Biarritz is the place.

right Bayonne by Garneray. Bayonne lies a few miles north of Biarritz, and is famous for its bullfights.

Molitg-les-Bains, in the Roussillon near the Spanish border, is one of the Barthélémy chain of spas. This shows the Grand Hotel Thermal where people follow the beauty treatments for which Molitg is famous.

The best surfing spots are on each side of the town, at the Côte des Basques and the Chambre d'Amour which has a charming name and a fitting legend. There was a rock grotto in the 'Room of Love' where two lovers became so oblivious of the world that they did not notice the tide was rising. They drowned, perhaps in each others' arms.

Biarritz has not less than five golf courses within a radius of twelve miles, and there is riding, bowling and ice skating. Nearby Bayonne has a mid-August festival, with bull races in the street. At the Park Mazon you may watch a fast ball game, called pelota. Wherever you go you will find Basque traditions, fine old churches, men wearing the black Basque beret, Basque dishes in the restaurants, especially the fisherman's *tioro* that resembles a *bouillabaisse*. It should be eaten in a small restaurant in the Old Port though even the Hotel de Palais offers a luxurious version to its luxurious guests.

Eugénie-les-Bains, two hours away by car, is a different story. It is a charming village built around hot springs which, according to what is un-doubtedly a legend, were discovered by Henri IV. How he got there, the legend does not explain. He called them Les Eaux de Saint-Loubouer. In 1745 an old château was built, surrounded by a park. One day in 1861 Empress Eugénie came there, and fell in love with the place. She spent many summers here and the spa called itself after her.

Now comes a modern switch. In Toulouse, not far away, in the 1950s a Frenchman began thinking about pollution and the hectic pace of life. He was working as a publicist in Paris and he hated the rat-race. Many people were running so hard that they had no time to learn the meaning of 'stress'. What these people needed (the Frenchman thought) were quiet out-of-the-way places where they could relax.

And thus M. Adrien Barthélémy began buying up forgotten spas here and there in France. The first was Molitg-les-Bains. The name is Arabic, Moorish or Catalan, pronounced 'Molitch'. It is near Prades, where Pablo Casals made his postwar home, not far from his native Catalonia. M. Barthélémy first bought the Grand Hotel Thermal, a medical and beauty estab-lishment – this is France, after all, where beauty is important – and then he acquired the Château de Riell, a hundred-year-old castle-like mansion. From the outside it was baroque and beautiful, but inside it was awful. It took his daughter Biche Barthélémy six years and much of her father's money to turn the old mansion into an elegant château for people in need of relaxa-tion. The entire inner structure had to be changed, a narrow elevator was installed, there is a small roof pool, and there is a lovely park surrounded by the hills of the Roussillion. The Spanish border and the small state of Andorra are not far away. The hot sulphurous springs of Molitg-les-Bains have been known for centuries for their salubrious effects on the skin. M. Barthélémy's experts discovered the exceptional health and beauty effects of the plankton, a sort of algae that grow near the hot springs. Now the delicate plankton is grown in complete darkness at 100 degrees Fahrenheit for twenty-one days. This also happens to be the cycle of a complete beauty cure, but there are shorter, eleven-day treatments for those who are already beautiful. Scientific research on the plankton, followed by commercial development, resulted in a line of the so-called Biotherm beauty products. They are now made in Monaco and sold everywhere. There are people who think that Molitg will become world famous, a spa for men and women who desire rejuvenation, beauty and relaxation in a Shangri-La atmosphere.

By the time the plankton's effects were discovered, Barthélémy had set up his Maison du Thermalisme in Paris, on the Avenue de l'Opéra, and owned the Chaîne Thermale de Soleil, five spas (all once forgotten) in southern France for people who want to lose weight, become more beautiful, or simply want to get away from it all. There is Gréoux-les-Bains in the Alpes de Haute-Provence, Saint-Christau in the Pyrenées, Barbotan-les-Thermes in the Armagnac region. All genuine spas with hot springs, doctors, nurses and all sorts of treatments.

My favourite is the one that called itself after Empress Eugénie. The château is called Les Prés et Les Sources d'Eugénie. Barthélémy, who has more spas than daughters, gave this one to his daughter Christine. It took her ten years to turn the elegant two-storey building into a number of luxurious duplexes. She left only the walls of the one-time Belle Epoque mansion which she restored in the style of the period. She put in beautiful dining rooms, intimate salons, harmonious colours, and when everything was ready, she rebuilt the old château that was identified with Eugénie.

The spa's thermal establishment – also available to guests staying in less expensive hotels in the village – is in a special wing. The springs are beneficial to people suffering from digestive ailments, gout, obesity. They come to the park three times a day, carrying their small drinking cups. It is much like Karlsbad (Karlovy Vary) in Czechoslovakia, but the cure in Eugénie-les-Bains is more restful and certainly less political. There is an old park with mimosas and planc trees, a small lake with Japanese-style bridges, lovely walks through the meadows with wild flowers and many herbs.

The best is yet to come. In 1972 Christine met Michel Guérard, who had yet to become the most famous avant-garde chef of *la nouvelle cuisine*. He ran his small restaurant in Asnières, a suburb of Paris. It was called Le Pot au Feu, and was becoming known among the city's gastronomes, but had to be torn down for a new street. Michel was so worried that he gained eighteen pounds in a few months; eventually he weighed 150 pounds and yet he is a short man, five feet three inches. First he took pills. That did not work. Then he tried not to eat at all, while trying to make *grande cuisine.* That almost drove him crazy. Finally he had the great idea of cooking *grande cuisine*, but omitting fats, flour, sauces and sugar.

It was in Eugénie-les-Bains that Michel Guérard, who had meanwhile married Christine, began to develop his famous menu *minceur*, fine cooking and few calories, not more than 400 or 450 a meal. Now Michel cooks his *minceur* things for well-to-do patients who go to the thermal establishments and submit to the rigorous treatment there. Within three weeks they are going to lose at least ten pounds, and all the time they will eat very well. It is a very strange cure but Christine thinks that people should have fun while they drink the waters and eat Michel's fine new things. She hopes the old clients will come back, they have come here for many years. She also wants the château to become a place for young people.

'Not necessarily young in years, but young in spirit, a place where something *happens*.' It will be as different as Michel Guérard's new way of cooking. One wonders what Empress Eugénie would have said to that.

Bad Ischl

The town of Bad Ischl, which lies in the Salzkammergut region, the 'salt chamber' of Austria, and where the saltwater baths have special healing powers.

Bad Ischl remains a charming anachronism, a real-life operetta. A good operetta contains dramatic, sad moments, and Ischl has had them. Anything may happen there and much still does. His Majesty, *der Kaiser*, spent eighty-three of his eighty-six summers there. There were many emperors during the six-hundred-year-long tenure of the Habsburg dynasty, but today only one is remembered as *the* emperor: Franz Joseph I. Early in July, when the hunting season started, the emperor would leave his Vienna residences, the Hofburg Palace and Castle Schönbrunn, and make the long journey to Ischl. Until 1877, when the railroad was built, it took four days to get there by coach. The emperor ruled over many lands, from Lake Garda in the west to Dalmatia in the south, the spas of Karlsbad and Marienbad in the north and the Carpathian mountains in the east. There were many beautiful spots in these countries where fifty-one million people spoke sixteen different languages. Franz Joseph made short visits there if it was absolutely necessary. But in summertime he went to Ischl to lead a strange, almost austere life that was dedicated to the almost 'pathological' pursuit of hunting. Why did he not visit the blue Adriatic, the glaciers and mountains of Tyrol, the dark woods of Poland? He went to Karlsbad where Goethe had spent so many summers, but he stayed only three days. The answer is his hunting passion that baffles even those Austrian historians who try to understand the emperor. The Kaiservilla, in the middle of the Kaiserpark, his summer residence, proves it.

When the Kaiser was in residence there, the villa was off limits, but nowadays tens of thousands of people walk up the gravel-covered avenue between finely cut hedges. The streetlamps on both sides are adorned with tiny imperial crowns in zinc. Eventually one stands before the façade which shows hunting motifs. It is a strange mixture of non-styles that does not deserve the name Biedermeier. The steep hill behind the villa, the Hainzen, was the emperor's private hunting domain. The halls and stairways of the villa, the large public rooms and small rooms have hunting trophies on the walls. Hundreds, thousands, tens of thousands of them, each with a notation giving place and day. In his sixty-six hunting summers Franz Joseph killed 2051 chamois and 1436 stags; all in all he killed 50,556 animals. Looking at the trophies one is reminded of the historians who claim that it was Franz Joseph who made Elisabeth unhappy (she called him 'Feldwebel', sergeant), who never tried to understand his gifted son, and who hated the Archduke Franz Ferdinand, the heir to the throne whose death in Sarajevo started the First World War which was the beginning of the end of the Habsburgs.

It was in this idyllic villa that Franz Joseph signed the ultimatum to Serbia which started the terrible chain reaction of two world wars. His desk is still in his writing room in the rear of the second floor, where he

Franz Joseph I (1830–1916), emperor of Austria. He spent every summer at Bad Ischl to pursue his love of hunting. The walls of the Kaiservilla at Bad Ischl are mounted with thousands of hunting trophies.

signed the fateful document on 28 July 1914. It was a formality: the ultimatum had been sent to Serbia the day before. The 'war party' at the Imperial Court had won, and the sinister Count Berchtold, the emperor's Foreign Minister, had arranged matters; he knew that the Monarchy was doomed, with no reliable friend in a very difficult situation. Did Franz Joseph, who was then eighty-four years old, go back hunting the next day? Perhaps.

Everybody in Austria knows about the imperial 'romance' between the emperor and 'die gnädige Frau', as she was officially called at the Court in Vienna, the actress Katharina Schratt. On 2 July 1908, Franz Joseph writes, 'My dear good friend! Just returned from an unsuccessful hunting day, and am informed that you arrive tonight . . .' He cannot see her the

The actress Katharina Schratt, Franz Joseph's greatest friend and confidante. She regularly stayed at Franz Joseph's Villa Felicitas which is next door to the Kaiservilla.

One of the salt-mining lakes, Hallstättersee, near Bad Ischl. Franz Joseph and his two brothers are still referred to as the 'Salzprinzen' – Salt princes – at the spa.

next morning, 'because I have ordered, in honour of the gentlemen, a hunt.'

A small garden door leads from the Kaiservilla to the nearby Villa Felicitas. 'Only two keys existed', a slightly scandalized chronicler reports. 'The Emperor kept one. The second he gave to Baroness Kiss, the actress better known by her professional name, Katharina Schratt.'

As a rule, Franz Joseph stayed there until 18 August, his birthday, then he returned to Vienna. His Court and everybody who considered himself somebody, stayed there with him. The Socialist-ruled, democratic Republic of Austria is almost sixty years old but elderly members of Vienna's 'society' still return from their vacations, in Ischl and elsewhere, after 18 August. An old habit is hard to break.

Every 18 August, there is a *Kaisermesse*, a Mass for the emperor, in the venerable parish church of St Nikolaus that dates from the Middle Ages, and has altar pieces painted in 1854 by Leopold Kupelwieser, a close friend of Franz Schubert.

I once attended the ceremony. The church was crowded with retired generals and elderly aristocratic ladies who greeted one another in a friendly, intimate way. Also present, and completely ignored by the Highnesses, were several Socialist councilmen who listened delightedly to a bellicose preacher who reminisced about the glory of the Monarchy that no longer is. Then the old imperial hymn was played, '*Gott erhalte, Gott beschütze unseren Kaiser, unser Land!*' (May God support and protect our Emperor, our Land!) The beautiful hymn taken from Joseph Haydn's *Kaiser*-Quartet is now taboo in Austria (though officially used by the West German Federal Republic), but it is much more stirring than the present republican hymn written by Mozart. The councilmen stood up, as did everybody else, and sang the hymn, which surprised no one in Ischl. 'Here *der Kaiser* still looks out of every window', a man said. As I wrote earlier, anything may happen in Ischl.

Franz Joseph may owe his birth to Ischl. The countryside has been known for over a thousand years; the first mention of the River Iscula (Ischl) is found in AD 829 in the Mondseer Charters. In 1262 there is a documentary notation of 'Iselen', and in 1392 the village of Ischl is said to be under the fort Wildenstein. Restricted space and poor soil forced the inhabitants to look for other work. There were the forests, the salt mine since 1563, the salt works opened seven years later, and the salt ships on the River Traun. The whole region became known as the Salzkammergut since it contained Austria's 'salt chamber', and salt meant power.

The healing powers of the Ischl mine were first discovered in 1819 by the saline physician Dr Joseph Götz. He first experimented with workers from the salt mine suffering from rheumatism and skin diseases. Götz was successful after adding a sulphur spring from the salt mine to the Ischl brine baths. Dr Götz, the discoverer of the spa, has only a memorial tablet in Ischl, but Dr Franz Wirer, Ritter von Rettenbach, has a proud monument in the Kurpark. No wonder. Dr Wirer was then personal physician to the imperial family. The family had a problem. In 1824 Archduke Franz Karl of Austria had married Princess Sophie, the nineteen-year-old daughter of King Maximilian of Bavaria. After some years they still had no children. What would happen to the dynasty?

At the suggestion of Dr Wirer, both a good spa physician and public relations expert, Sophie hopefully went to Ischl to take hot saltwater baths.

Two years later, in 1830, Franz Joseph was born. He and his two younger brothers, Maximilian and Karl Ludwig, are still called *Salzprinzen*, the Salt Princes, in Ischl. Their parents liked the place and went there every summer. It is said, that Franz Joseph fell in love with Ischl at the age of three. During his long, hard life he was always happy to escape from the Spanish court ceremonial in Vienna into the bucolic hunting atmosphere of Ischl. Dr Wirer meanwhile created the Esplanade along the River Traun, a fashionable promenade that was to remind the visitors of Vienna. The baths were built, a drinking hall, the Kurpark, and in no time the members of the Court and Vienna's society deserted Baden near Vienna and came to Ischl for the season.

It was in Ischl, at the Hotel Austria, on the Esplanade, that the Tenth Court Ball was held on 17 August 1853, when the young emperor – he had mounted the throne in 1848, at the age of eighteen – met the Bavarian princesses Helene and Elisabeth. He was supposed to marry the older girl, Helene, but as every Austrian knows: he fell in love with the sixteen-year-old younger sister, his cousin Elisabeth, the romantic 'Sissi'. Princess Helene ('Nene') did not exist anymore, but she did not mind. She had no wish to be the empress, she loved someone else. The designs of Franz Joseph's domineering mother had misfired. However, the parents gave Franz Joseph the Kaiservilla as a present, and for the next sixty years Ischl became the rendezvous of the Great World.

Emperors and kings, ministers and soldiers made the pilgrimage to the Imperial Villa. Wilhelm I, the German Emperor, came several times, also the Emperor of Brazil, the Kings of Serbia, Denmark, Rumania, Greece, Bulgaria and Siam. Edward VII of England came in 1905, 1907 and 1908. By that time Franz Joseph was a bitter, unhappy man. His marriage to Elisabeth had been very unhappy. Their oldest child, Crown Prince Rudolf, had died in Mayerling. The lovely Empress did not like Vienna and spent much time in Hungary and Ireland. In 1898 she was stabbed to death near Geneva by the Italian anarchist Luccheni. Franz Joseph, who had always loved her, was terribly shaken, and it did not help that Katharina Schratt became elusive at a time when he might have needed her.

At his villa in Ischl the emperor was informed one day in 1866 that his armies had been defeated by the Prussians, and in the summer of 1916 he said, 'I won't stand for it, I am going to make peace.' He did not have the chance. He died on 21 November. He was and remained a man of the nineteenth century.

But between 1853 and 1914 Ischl – in 1906 it was renamed Bad Ischl to denote its status as a health resort – was simply *the* place in Europe during a few weeks in summer, *the* status symbol of the Belle Epoque. After the Imperial Family went there, followed by the aristocracy and the rich arrivistes, there came the artists, composers, writers, painters, and the inevitable hangers-on. Ambitious young soubrettes hoped to be discovered for a theatre in Vienna, or at least by a dashing archduke. Ischl was then Biarritz, Deauville, Montecatini and Marienbad rolled into one. In Ischl, in 1908, you could watch *the* emperor and King Edward VII of England riding in an automobile, the only time Franz Joseph stepped into such a contraption. (He also ignored the newly invented telephone; he was smart.) And after a state affair, His Majesty would happily put on his Styrian suit and walk with his gamekeeper through the woods.

My mother once asked my father to take her to Ischl for 'the season', and he sadly shook his head. Impossible he said, he could not even get a room there. In Ischl a twenty-one-carat duchess was glad to have a small *Kabinett*, without bath. The VIPs whom the Emperor did not want to have at his villa, were put up at the leading hotel, the Post (still owned by the great-grandson of the founder, Herr Franz Koch).

Bad Ischl had its share of famous devotees. Johannes Brahms spent twelve summers there. He ate his beloved goulash at the Hotel Elisabeth or the *spécialité de la maison* at David Sonnenschein's kosher restaurant. Johann Strauss loved Ischl because it was (and is) always raining there. The Salzkammergut is as well-known for its *Schnürlregen*, 'rain that comes down as in strings', a quiet and steady rain that soothes the nerves, as for its deep-blue lakes and deep-green meadows. In Italy they call it spaghetti rain, it comes down slowly and perhaps depressingly, but it is never depressing in Ischl. 'A perfect holiday', Strauss wrote to Alexander Girardi, the celebrated comedian. 'Always rain, the sound of the brook, and a well-heated room where I can write music.' Girardi understood. He was from Graz in Styria, and in Ischl he had learned the trade of a locksmith. He became a very great actor in Vienna because he understood people and he learned to perform the part of a Viennese that every Viennese would like to be. 'If I had been born there, I could never do it,' he said.

The great Austrian poet Nikolaus Lenau once wrote in Ischl, '*Himmel! schon vierzehn Tage unablässig, bist du gehässig und regennässig*' (Good Heavens, fourteen days with no let-up, you've been hateful and wet with rain.) Lenau

A state dinner in honour of Edward VII at the Imperial Villa of Bad Ischl on 15 August 1907. Edward and Franz Joseph are in the centre of the picture at the top of the table. Hunting trophies cover the wall behind them.

got depressed by the rain but he was easily depressed and later died in a state of insanity.

The poet Adalbert Stifter, the poets and playwrights Franz Grillparzer and Johann Nestroy, the composers Giacomo Meyerbeer and Otto von Nicolai all came to Ischl. As did the painters Rudolf von Alt, Thomas Ender and Ferdinand Georg Waldmüller, who are now being rediscovered. But the most famous composer in Ischl today is the late Franz Lehár. In some circles he is better known than *the* emperor, and many people come to Ischl to look at the Lehár villa, not the Kaiservilla. Lehár wrote his masterpiece, *The Merry Widow*, and twenty-three other operettas in Ischl. His once beautiful house, three stories high, full of memorabilia, stands on the Esplanade. On the other side of the river is the house of Richard Tauber, Lehár's favourite tenor. Lehár loved Bad Ischl and died there in 1948. By that time people had forgotten that Richard Wagner with his *Meistersinger* and Lehár were Hitler's favourite composers. Lehár has a cenotaph at the Ischl cemetery, and there are always fresh flowers on his grave. He has a monument at the Kurpark, and his house is now a museum, located at the Lehár Quai. On the top floor is a Biedermeier room where one sees Lehár's talisman, a small brown elephant. He always carried it in his pocket, when he conducted or listened to the world première of a new work. The celebrated villa is a rather gloomy building overlooking the river. It is a hallowed place; no sardonic remarks will be tolerated. There are people in Ischl that consider the spa's 'operetta festival' superior to the Salzburg festival. During these weeks there are Lehár lectures, Lehár memorial services, and Lehár pictures in the stores. Lehár has become the Mozart of Ischl, the former court theatre is now named after him, and he has escaped the ultimate indignity: in Salzburg the Mozartkugeln are called after the composer, but in Ischl no pastry has been named after Lehár.

Ischl was always a musically-minded town, and many composers felt at home there. Nowadays five brass bands compete; the most famous of them, the Salinen-Orchestra, was originally made up of employees of the salt mines. Few employees of the mines now play in the orchestra but the Tuesday evening concert of the Salinen-Orchestra is an important musical and social event in Ischl. During the summer, when Lehár is always being performed here, admirers approach his house, the 'museum', to admire English Biedermeier pieces, Bohemian glass, Venetian chandeliers, a vase donated by Tauber, a Rembrandt and the photographs of the Master, showing him with Lotte Lehmann, Frau Anna Sacher, and his wife. His golden conductor's baton is also there, in the room where he died. Even the small bottles with medicaments are there. In Ischl, they do not remove things, they leave everything as it was. Not so bad in the case of Lehár, but terrible in the case of Franz Joseph I.

Franz Lehár, the Hungarian composer of *The Merry Widow* and many other operettas, lived at Bad Ischl in what has become known as the Lehár-villa for most of his life.

The Kaiservilla was not taken over by the Republic but remains the property of the Habsburg family. For a long time it belonged to Archduke Hubert Salvator, and now it belongs to his children. There were thirteen children – the Habsburg believe in descendants – and every time one of them got married, the family would take over the villa for a week. Relatives and friends arrived, cooks and servants were hired, and the place was crowded with highnesses. There would be a ceremony at the church, where a marble plate reminds you that 'Court organist Anton Bruckner played the organ here at festive occasions of the Imperial House.'

In Vienna's Hofburg the emperor's private table service is shown, glittering with golden vases, crystal goblets, precious china, gleaming silver. It expresses the pomp and the pomposity of the absolute monarchy. Guests were often frustrated though by the sacred rule that forbade them to touch their food the moment the emperor had finished his. His Majesty was naturally served first, and he was a fast eater. The younger archdukes would be served very late, and no matter how hard they tried, time was always running out when the liveried footmen served them the tempting dishes. They swallowed as much of the food as they could, but almost as soon as they had started the emperor would finish, and they were obliged to also. No wonder they were still hungry, and ran to the Hotel Sacher, ordering

The Kaiservilla, where Franz Joseph I entertained great leaders of the world, and where he signed the ultimatum to Serbia which started the terrible chain reaction leading to two world wars.

Zauner's restaurant, Bad Ischl, where artists, composers and writers once met. It is still renowned for its delicious pastries.

a substantial meal that no one would spoil for them. In Ischl, however, there was not much etiquette. The Kaiser was happy in the evening with a glass of sour milk and a piece of dark peasant bread. It is not known when he ate the good pastries made by Zauner. He never went there. The great pastry shop would send its delicacies to the Kaiservilla when the emperor was in residence.

Zauner was founded in 1832. It was then known as Café Walther. By that time the famous Demel's in Vienna was already a forty-six-year-old institution. In 1869 the son of Johannes Zauner, Karl, moved into today's building in the narrow Pfarrgasse which is always crowded with people and cars. But all is forgotten as one walks into Zauner's sweet oasis. It is not a large place. A front room with the counters and shelves and a few tables. The *Rauchsalon* behind it, where smoking is permitted. And in the rear is the Small Salon. The decor is intimately golden, known locally as 'imperial style', not to be confused with French Empire. The atmosphere is discreetly Biedermeier. Less American English and more nasal-aristocratic Maria Theresa Austrian – 'g'sehn' instead of gesehen, the first syllables are swallowed – is spoken at Zauner's than at Demel's. Elderly habitués, dressed somewhat shabbily in *fin-de-siècle* fashion, converse in the dialect artfully used by Hofmannsthal in the first act of *Der Rosenkavalier*. A few years ago one could see the *Kaiserdirndl*, if one was lucky, a dignified old lady who in the old, old days had been invited to the Schratt villa in the presence of His Majesty. She would never, *never*, tell you what had been said even if she had remembered. In that respect she was like Frau Schratt who died at the age of eighty-six and refused to write her memoirs, turning down some fabulous offers. It would be difficult to find such a lady today.

Zauner's should not be compared with Demel's. The Austrians are lucky to have both. Demel's may be more refined, big-city style, but Zauner's is more solid, the emperor's spa. The artists and composers and writers would meet at Zauner's, greet one another cordially or with well performed cordiality, and start gossiping about those not present. Demel's was mostly a pastry shop, a *Konditorei*, but Zauner's remained a coffee house. Prominent habitués had 'their' tables. The operetta composers would hold court. Ischl was always the operetta capital of Austria. Lehár, Leo Fall, Oskar Straus (one s, no relation to either Johann or Richard), who wrote *Walzertraum*, Emmerich Kálmán (*Die Czardasfürstin*), Ralph Benatzky, Edmund Eysler, Robert Stolz; all came to Zauner's in the afternoon, surrounded by their librettists, publishers, admirers and hangers-on. One wonders how many operettas were concocted around a *Zaunerstollen*, a *Zaunerkipfel* and a *Zaunertorte*, the great speciality of the house.

Zaunerstollen is a nougat made with ground hazelnuts and almonds, crumbled *Oblaten* and grated chocolate. It was invented eighty years ago by Viktor Zauner and is still made according to the 'secret' recipe. At Zauner's they also make *Oblaten*, round wafers filled with sugar and ground almonds that were originally invented in the spa of Karlsbad. *Zaunerkipfel* are puff-pastry croissants filled with ground nuts. These specialties cannot be described, they must be tasted. There is also a rich assortment of conventional Schnitten, Rouladen (including the rich, red Cardinal Roulade), Torten, *Ischlertörtchen*, and a very good *Topfentorte*, a cheese cake. The *Malakofftorte* is a poem written in whipped cream. During the season the Torten are filled with fresh berries; the finest is the *Erdbeertorte*, filled with freshly picked wild strawberries, very expensive. It is no secret that some people

drive to Ischl to enjoy an afternoon meal – *Jause* – at Zauner's and they do not even look at the Kaiservilla or the Lehárvilla.

Nowadays they also serve a mini-lunch at Zauner's, the best in Ischl or, for that matter, in the entire Salzkammergut. Homemade chicken or oxtail soup, cold chicken, delicious sandwiches, a very good *ragout fin*, a light omelet, a warm *Schinkenkipferl*, a baked croissant filled with chopped ham. Excellent coffee, very good service. By the time the lunch people leave, the dainty old ladies are there, all set for the afternoon gossip, and plump women tourists from Germany who should not even look at Zauner's pastry, eating double portions of *Malakofftorte*. At the old railway station where His Majesty arrived each summer after 1877, I asked the stationmaster whether there had been a special ceremonial for the arrival of the monarch.

'Not that I know of, but I wasn't there, it's such a long time ago. I was told they would put down a red carpet, which they do now in luxury hotels all over the world when they have special guests, not an emperor. He walked through a narrow corridor, and got into his *fiaker*.' A coach drawn by two horses. 'Or two local men would carry him up to the villa in a sedan. I saw an old picture the other day.'

A few years ago they needed the space of the old corridor and built the stationmaster's office with the signal board there. Exactly where His Majesty had stepped out into the street the wall is now decorated with the official portrait of the President of the Republic of Austria.

An early drawing of Bad Ischl showing the River Traun and stately mansions. The flat-bottomed boats on the river were used for the shallow stretches along the salt route.

Bad Gastein

The beautiful mountain resort, Bad
Gastein, where the Gasteiner Ache
cascades down the rocks and through
the town.

Bad Gastein, also known as Badgastein or simply Gastein, especially to old hands and local people, has become many things to many men. It is, above all, a beautiful mountain resort, at an altitude of 3570 feet above sea level, a magnificent amphitheatre formed by evergreen slopes on both sides of the Gasteiner Ache, a blue-white mountain stream rushing down 600 feet deep in spectacular torrents and waterfalls. Owing to its location, Bad Gastein has some of the tallest hotels in Europe, certainly the tallest in the Alps, fourteen-floor structures built deeply into the granite rocks. At night the tall buildings look like a stretch of New York's skyline that has been magically transplanted into Austria's Hohe Tauern.

Many places in Austria are internationally known for their ski runs. It is not generally known that Bad Gastein is Austria's most important winter sports resort. Since the last war, many championships have been held here, in 1958 the Alpine World Ski Championships, in 1967 the Alpine Cup. A two-section cable railway goes up to the Stubnerkogel (7350 feet), and several ski lifts take skiers to the Graukogel, 'only' 6525 feet high. There are family slopes and standard slopes for almost everybody, and there are racing slopes laid out for men and women. The slope for men is an almost continuous descent from the summit to the valley station. The Blaukaar slope is known as 'difficult', which is an understatement. Ambitious skiers hire a guide and go up all the way to the glaciers. Pedestrians gaze at the glaciers and lofty peaks from below, which can be just as nice and is safer. And they live longer.

To make you live longer is the true purpose of Bad Gastein. Called 'the source of youth', Gastein has been a spa and convalescent centre for the past six hundred years. It is said to be unique because its healing characteristics are based on natural resources which include eighteen world-famous springs, with a temperature between 97 and 110 degrees Fahrenheit, which are piped into a hundred odd places in the spa. In Gastein you do not have to go to a bathhouse to get the treatment, the waters come to your hotel. Many people are deeply convinced that the waters of Gastein have cured their ills, made them feel young again, and given them a longer lease of life.

The fabulous waters are clear, colourless, odourless and tasteless. But they contain lithium, manganese, phosphoric acid, fluorine, cesium and a little, very little arsenic. The water also contains from 120 to 300 Mache units of radium per litre. These radioactive springs, when used in the right dosage, have a rejuvenating effect on the growth of cells and on the hormonal system. This sounds a little like the dubious newspaper ads, 'Get Young Fast', but scientists have carried out all sorts of experiments to prove the effect of the waters. The healing Radon gas quickly separates from the water and enriches the air in the bathing cabin which acts as an inhalatorium. Hundreds of tests have been carried out by the research institute of the Austrian Academy of Sciences and by the University Clinic at Innsbruck which has a field station in Bad Gastein.

It was noted that little frogs kept in thermal water grew twice as fast as frogs kept in the same ordinary water at the same temperature. Sexual maturity appeared sooner in animals that were kept in thermal water. Strangely, the waters lose no radioactivity on their six-mile journey to Bad Hofgastein, which is farther north, where they are taken through an ingenious piping system. Thus the same cure is available at lower prices in Bad Hofgastein, perhaps in less fashionable, more rustic surroundings; but naturally no one talks about this in Bad Gastein, even though they talk about everything else.

The doctors, especially; they point out that the atmosphere of the mountain spa carries a high, negative, electric charge which increases the percentage of ultraviolet rays in the sunshine. The air is pure, unpolluted and almost always free from fog (though it rains a great deal). Even people who do not take the baths inhale as much radium-emanation in the course of the day there as a bather absorbs in half an hour.

No sooner had this fact become confirmed than Bad Gastein appointed itself as an ideal congress centre. It was pointed out that visitors would meet in an ideal, stimulating atmosphere. They would be working hard and getting younger in the process. The Kongresshaus and the Congress Centre in the Haus Austria now accommodates thirteen hundred people in congress halls and conference rooms. Participants are told that they do something for their health, which is unusual, *and* for their career.

What happens to people like the natives of Bad Gastein, who spend their lives there, exposed to continuous radiation? Atomic age optimists claim that the local people whose families have lived there for generations absorb more gamma rays every day than worriers all over the world who complain that we are all being killed in slow doses by nuclear tests. They say that if the pessimists were right, the Gasteiners would have been burned to death a long time ago, yet they are still going strong.

But the local authorities take no chances. 'In accordance with current legal requirements, thermal baths may only be taken with a doctor's prescription', it says, and to make it even more clear, 'A *local* doctor will be required to verify any cases where patients have prescriptions from foreign doctors.' To become a *Kurgast* of good standing you have to see a spa doctor and must get his permission. Otherwise you may arrive in the spa sanctum and be told that it is not for you. Chances are that you will be permitted to take the cure unless you suffer from fever, a heart defect, heart muscle disease, cancer and other malignant tumours, tuberculosis or mental disease. Many doctors elsewhere are cautious about sending their patients to

A nineteenth-century watercolour of Bad Gastein and the surrounding Alps.

Bad Gastein. They explain that the powerful Radon emanation may make basically healthy people feel younger and healthier – but that they may also 'wake up' latent diseases that were not known and may never have become known without the powerful radiation of Bad Gastein. Thus, a wise doctor tells you, 'When in doubt, don't go there.'

This is not what the spa doctors tell you. They point at the list of illnesses that have been successfully treated in Bad Gastein. All rheumatic complaints, circulatory problems, the prevention of heart infarcts, impotence and infertility, premature ageing, gout, kidney stones, after-treatment of broken bones, asthma and bronchitis and paradentosis. It sounds like a fairy tale but miracles have happened in Bad Gastein. They also happen in Lourdes. In both cases the main thing is *to believe*. Some people go to Bad Gastein every year and always feel better afterwards because they believe in it. The spa doctors often repeat the old motto that prevention is better than cure. They advise you to come there even when you are perfectly healthy.

Experience has shown that the bath treatment has the best effects after twelve to twenty-one baths. Twenty-one baths are said to be the optimum. Some people, however, are required to stay from four to six weeks. In contrast to other fashionable spas, there is no nonsense about the baths in Gastein. You are told to report at an early hour to the bath attendant of your hotel. Insomniacs may start as early as 4 a.m. and some do. The baths are located in the basement of the hotels, and the cure can be taken all year round, in winter as well as in summer. Local etiquette demands that you do not recognize other bathers in the elevator, even the charming lady – probably looking less charming now – that you were dancing with a couple of hours ago.

Your bath is probably a somewhat old-fashioned, tiled affair containing 200 gallons of the miraculous, radioactive waters. The bath is built into the floor. You walk down a few steps and sit or lie in the waters like a Roman emperor. You may increase the effect by underwater massage, using the strong jet of water from a rubber hose. Do not do it unless the doctor authorizes you to do it.

There is a clock on the wall and a thermometer giving the exact temperature of the water. Usually you start out with fifteen minutes at 95 degrees Fahrenheit. Old Gastein books call this the 'conductive temperature'. It may seem pretty hot to you, and toward the end of the fifteen-minute period you will find yourself glancing anxiously, even impatiently at the clock. Later on, the temperature of the water may go up to 100 degrees Fahrenheit and the duration of the bath to thirty minutes. The baths are expensive, and some people like to stay in 'a little longer' to get their money's worth.

Do not do it. The waters strongly affect the heart even if you do not

MINERAL SPRINGS
OF
GERMANY, AUSTRIA, AND
SWITZERLAND.
WITH
NOTES ON CLIMATIC RESORTS AND CONSUMPTION SANITARIUMS
PEAT, MUD, AND SAND BATHS, WHEY AND GRAPE CURES, &c.
A POPULAR MEDICAL GUIDE.

BY EDWARD GUTMANN, M.D.

With Illustrations, Comparative Tables, and a Coloured Map, explaining the Situation, and Chemical Composition of the Spas.

In balneis salus.

London:
SAMPSON LOW, MARSTON, SEARLE, & RIVINGTON.
New York:
D. APPLETON AND COMPANY.
1880.
[*All rights reserved.*]

The frontispiece of a popular medical guide to the spas of Germany, Austria and Switzerland. Bad Gastein's world-famous mineral springs are known as 'the source of youth' because they are said to have a rejuvenating effect.

notice it at once. In other spas around the world one follows or does not follow the prescription of the spa doctor; no great harm will result. Bad Gastein is special. The radioactive water is too powerful to fool around with. In the old days, some people had breakfast served in the bath, and others were said to have played cards there, the longer they stayed in the better (they thought.) After such activities, some former patients were carried out to the local cemetery. Bad Gastein has been a miracle for some, but it is no joke.

After the bath, you rub yourself with a wet towel and lie down on a couch in the bath-chamber, inhaling the air which is full of radio-emanation. This part of the cure is very important. Again: do not stay longer than you are told.

Then you take the elevator again and go back to your room for rest or sleep, and you have breakfast, the best meal of the day. Strong coffee that has been a specialty of Austria since the wars against the Turks, crisp rolls called *Kaisersemmeln*, not called after the Kaiser, but because they were invented around 1730, during the reign of Charles VI, by a Viennese baker named Kayser. Originally it was known as *Kaysersemmel* but in Vienna all good things, such as Johann Strauss's *Kaiserwalzer* and the good *Kaiserwein* were sooner or later dedicated to an emperor. A genuine *Kaisersemmel* is still kneaded with the fingers, it cannot be made by machines, and is more expensive than an ordinary *Semmel*. In Bad Gastein some bakers still make the real article but for how long no one dares predict. Butter, marmalade, jam is served with the rolls, and there are various extras.

Some people get dressed and go up to one of the nearby mountain inns for breakfast. Years ago I would climb the pine forests to the Café Windischgrätzhöhe to enjoy breakfast with a magnificent view of the Gastein valley. In those days they made their own butter and cream in the house dairy, and they had fine eggs. Their scrambled eggs, known as *Eierspeis*, were the answer to a genuine French *omelette nature*.

The rest of the day is yours, that is the beauty of the cure. Many local doctors advise slow walks – the emphasis is on slow – and 'mild' exercise which is said to enhance the effect of the cure. Above all, they tell you not to expect too much too soon. People who have been to Gastein for twenty years and swear by it – such people exist – claim that the cure shows its full effect only after six months.

'It's hard to explain', an elderly man told me. 'All of a sudden I feel less tired and more active than in a long time. I sleep better. I feel like walking, doing things. I was in Gastein during the summer and around Christmas I am beginning to feel the effect. It's a fact, it isn't my imagination.'

Though Bad Gastein is very old – so are most European spas with thermal

The Gastein valley. Hofgastein, Bad Gastein's sister town, is in the foreground, whereas Bad Gastein lies behind further up the valley.

springs – it is also a very 'modern' recreation resort, a paradise for over-worked executives and victims of high-pressure living. As long as they follow their doctor's prescription. One *Kurarzt*, as persuasive about the spa as the rest of his colleagues, explains, 'The effect of the cure consists in the acceleration of metabolism. It stimulates the formation of blood, influences the blood circulation, and the functioning of the heart. The pulse becomes slower and stronger, increased blood pressure is reduced. The baths also have an effect on the vegetative part of the nervous system and stimulate the sexual glands. Thus the Bad Gastein cure is nearly everybody's answer to fatigue and nervous exhaustion. Specifically, it does wonders for people who suffer from troubles of metabolism and old-age phenomena, and from disturbances of the endocrine glands. We managed to cure people who came here with functional depressions. We've had victims of sciatica, paralysis and arteriosclerosis. Some came to Gastein hobbling on two sticks and before they left they went up to the waterfall and threw them in. They walked without difficulty after the cure.'

I have never met anyone who arrived with two sticks and later threw them into the waterfall, but the story is often told in Bad Gastein and I have talked to people who claim they knew such people. As I said, the first prerequisite of every cure is to believe in it. A great many people come here year after year and they say they would no longer be alive without the waters of the spa.

Some very sick people are permitted a new form of therapy, the emanation and heating in the Gastein thermal tunnel (the so-called *Heilstollen* in nearby Böckstein). There the radium-emanation (Radon) is particularly strong, an average of $4,1.10^{-9}$ Curies per litre of tunnel air in the various therapy areas. The temperature inside the tunnel increases from 37·2 degrees Celsius in the first therapy station to 41·6 degrees Celsius in the hottest station. The relative humidity is 90 to 97 per cent. The *Stollen* is the only hot-air emanatorium in the world with an overall dimension of 20,000 cubic metres. It is used for the treatment – always under strict medical care – of almost desperate cases that could not be cured by the waters of Bad Gastein. But the combination of heat and the inhalation of Radon are said to create veritable miracles. The patients are taken into the tunnel which stretches far into the mountain on small cars that stop at the various stations. There they lie down in the heat and humidity. I have never been inside the tunnel. The cure is said to be hell – but the patients pray it may help and it has helped. Radon passes out of the body within a few hours without leaving any after effects at all. The doctors are convinced there is no danger caused by the rays during the treatment. The tunnel is open from the middle of February to the middle of October. Patients apply to the Gasteiner Heilstollen, or to the spa management

Taking the therapeutic radium treatment in the Gastein thermal tunnel, Heilstollen. The combination of heat, humidity and high radium-emanation is said to have miraculous results.

in Bad Gastein. Many tests are prescribed before a person is accepted.

Despite these forbidding details, Gastein is beautiful and never dull. Many people go there without taking the cure. In the summer, there is golf, riding, swimming, mountaineering; in winter time there are all winter sports. All year long there is the pure, stimulating air. The place is about sixty miles south of Salzburg, from where a fascinating mountain road leads to Bad Gastein, and there is a daily bus service all year round. Fast express trains from Western Europe and from Greece and Yugoslavia stop at Bad Gastein. All summer long there are flights to Salzburg from New York via Brussels, Frankfurt and London. Salzburg Festival visitors who feel the stress of a modern festival often go to Gastein to recuperate.

Horsedrawn coaches with loquacious coachmen are available who tell you at the drop of a good tip how they took Kaiser Franz Joseph I and Kaiser Wilhelm of Germany to the Grüner Baum, or some other forest café serving the afternoon snack known as *Jause*, with *Guglhupf*. It may not be true but you asked for it. The spa orchestra gives daily concerts. It has fewer strings than the Vienna Philharmonic but its programmes are more ambitious, and major symphonies are performed with minor casts.

Ambition has always been the keynote of Bad Gastein. The casino offers roulette, baccarat and black jack. It is a modest affair compared to Monte Carlo and Baden-Baden but the croupiers make up for it by their extravagant manners and they tell you there are often more millionaires and film stars in Bad Gastein than in Monte Carlo, 'where one doesn't get younger'. The combination of having a good time and 'getting younger' by the minute seems unbeatable.

Gastein has been known since the Middle Ages. The Roman emperors missed the hot springs, though bronze coins of the Emperors Trajan and Severus were found in the valley. But the first documentary mention occurred relatively late, at the end of the tenth century. Local historians claim that the parish church was built around AD 696 though this cannot be proven. The St Maria Church in Hofgastein, Badgastein's less affluent sister, is mentioned in a document dated 2 August 1023, as *ecclesia parochialis in Castun*. During the following centuries there were numerous arguments

Horsedrawn coaches await passengers arriving by train at Gastein station in 1903.

Emperor Franz Joseph of Austria and Kaiser Wilhelm I of Germany visiting Bad Gastein; their foreign ministers often held conferences there. When Wilhelm I died Gastein sent a wreath made of 3000 Edelweiss flowers.

and fights between the dukes of Bavaria and the Archbishop of Salzburg who claimed to rule the valley of Gastein. The revolts of the peasants, the wars against the Turks and the Thirty Years' War affected the remote valley. In 1525, the people of Gastein rebelled against the Archbishop. A local man, Kaspar Prassler, led his men to Salzburg and occupied the town. Archbishop Lang withdrew to the Fortress Hohensalzburg. Eventually a peace treaty was signed but the peasants started a second revolt in 1526. It ended disastrously and twenty-seven leaders of the revolt, among them eight from Gastein, were executed. The plague came to the valley in 1528, and 350 inhabitants died. Then came the Thirty Years' War. A great many people in the valley had joined the Protestants; even the Jesuits were unable to prevent this. Eventually many Gasteiners were forced to go into exile. In 1731, more than 480 of them were sent to East Prussia.

The valley of Gastein suffered a great deal during the Napoleonic wars. After the peace treaty of Schönbrunn in 1809 the Austrians ceded Salzburg and Gastein to Bavaria. Eventually the country was given back to Austria. 'The revolution of 1848 created no echo in the valley of Gastein.' The little known wild spa became a world spa. The Prussian Field Marshal Moltke came to Gastein in 1859 and told Wilhelm, then King of Prussia, about his 'discovery'. Wilhelm was an enthusiastic spa visitor; so are most Germans. Under the pseudonym Graf von Zollern (he also used it when he went to Karlsbad) he came to Gastein in 1863, and then again in the following two years. On 14 August 1865 the Treaty of Gastein was signed in the Hotel Straubinger. Holstein would be administrated by Austria, Schleswig by Prussia. When Wilhelm I became Kaiser of Germany, he returned to Bad Gastein; he came there twenty times and told everybody that the thermal springs had done him a great deal of good.

Eventually Wilhelm I used to meet Franz Joseph in Gastein and their Foreign Ministers had long conferences there. Bismarck stayed at the Schwaigerhaus, Julius Count Andrássy at the Straubinger (which still exists). The two emperors met for the last time in 1886. The German Kaiser, ninety years old, had brought along his grand-child, who later became Kaiser Wilhelm II. When he died in 1888, Gastein sent a wreath made of 3000 Edelweiss flowers to his funeral.

The Austrian Empress Elisabeth came five times, between 1888 and 1893, and is still remembered locally at the Kaiserin-Elisabeth-Promenade. A great many emperors and kings came to Bad Gastein prior to the First World War. The Tauern Railroad that was opened in 1909 brought a great many patients to Gastein. Then came the world wars. At the end of 1945 American troops occupied Bad Gastein and some luxury hotels became luxury G.I. billets. The Americans moved out around 1950 and ever since Bad Gastein has been a world-renowned health resort.

It should be added that Theophrastus Paracelsus, the medical practitioner, came here in 1562 to study the thermal springs but the people were not interested. The big local business was then gold and silver mining. Perhaps the ores were the reason why the Archbishop of Salzburg showed such interest in Gastein. The supply of gold dried up during the eighteenth century, but the springs did not. The waters have stopped flowing only once, in 1906, for twenty-four hours, when an earthquake was rocking Lisbon, a thousand miles away. The panic in Gastein was almost as great as it was in Lisbon.

In the nineteenth century everybody who was anybody came to Gastein. Franz Schubert probably wrote his *Gasteiner Symphony* here which remains lost and has become a major enigma in the composer's life. Prior to the last war, when the Salzburg Festival became famous, Toscanini, Bruno Walter and Thomas Mann came here almost every year. After the war, Bad Gastein changed its face almost every year. After the French and the American soldiers moved out, there was the arrival of French and Italian black marketeers, and old Gasteiners remember with a slight shudder that the season was 'very noisy'. Eventually, the Germans became rich, prosperous and suffered from stress and it was inevitable that they should rediscover Bad Gastein, many years after the emperors had been here. They came in their large Mercedes cars – the spa built the Parkhaus at the waterfall with a capacity for 400 cars – and they worked hard to be cured of the 'manager's disease'.

The composer Franz Schubert who often visited Gastein and was inspired by it to write the Gasteiner symphony.

When I first came to Bad Gastein in 1950, there were some luxury hotels that now no longer exist. The Europe was an old-fashioned palace where one got lost in the spacious corridors. The Astoria was so elegant that it did not bother to advertise its rates. The Kaiserhof, on the other side of the Ache, still exists, with its large private park. The Bellevue has become a de-luxe hotel, and also the Elisabethpark. But there are about a hundred hotels, pensions, inns and private homes, catering to every taste and purse. Many hotels stay open from May to October and during a short winter season, but a few hotels stay open all year and these are the ones I prefer. The service is more reliable and the cuisine less erratic than in the big houses when the kitchen brigade reaches the top of its form just toward the end of the season.

One of the good things about Bad Gastein is the lack of any prescribed diet. With the exception of a few people who demand a certain diet, especially among the diet-conscious Germans, everybody may eat what he likes. Many people like to dine at night in a Stüberl, located in the basement of several hotels, where the mood is less formal than in the splendid dining room. These are wood-panelled restaurants with wrought-iron lamps, zither-players, and waitresses in dirndls. The menu is always enormous, with several kinds of goulash and the tried-and-true Viennese specialties, such as *Wiener Schnitzel*, *Zwiebelrostbraten* and the inevitable *Salzburger Nockerln*. If you managed to avoid them in Salzburg, you will get them in Bad Gastein.

Many regions are represented on the menu but not Gastein. No one has bothered to invent a *Gasteinerbraten* or a *Gasteinerschnitte*. Strange because the most celebrated Austrian cook, Eckart Witzigmann, was born in Bad Gastein and started his career at the Hotel Straubinger. Witzigmann does not practise in Austria, however, but in Munich, where he is comfortably surrounded by ample supplies of good products and affluent clients who like first-class food and do not mind paying for it.

But the zither-players in Gastein will not let you down, and there is folklore entertainment, and there are several night clubs with charming Austrians who look like operetta princes. Romanticists may go up to the Bellevue Alm to dance under the stars. Serious opera fans may take a train to Salzburg to listen to a Festival performance. But whatever you do, do not forget that you have a date with your bath attendant down in the basement, at six o'clock in the morning.

Bad Ragaz

A warm spring was discovered in the
Tamina gorge at Bad Ragaz in 1240
and wooden steps were constructed
into the water for patients to bathe
there. This shows the dramatic gorge
and the precarious pathway which has
been hewn into the rock.

Super-highways are useful for drivers who want to go somewhere fast and do not otherwise care how they get there. All they see is the scenery either side of the road and a few petrol stations. Years ago, before the Swiss built the autobahn from Zürich to the Engadin, a motorist driving on the narrow road from Zürich to Chur (and then up to Sankt Moritz) would pass through Bad Ragaz. All of a sudden, the conservative Swiss landscape with signs of BANK, CHANGE, GASTHOF, HOTEL seemed to disappear, and for a few seconds one drove past luxurious hotels, a deep green golf course, a Kursaal-Casino. People would walk over well-tended paths. Time seemed to stand still in this small, lovely spa. Then it was gone, one saw the next CHANGE sign on the way to Chur, and one no longer thought about it. One wanted to be in Sankt Moritz in time for lunch or dinner.

It never occurred to me that I might go to Bad Ragaz myself. The Swiss are not as spa conscious as the Germans who believe that there is a spa for every sickness. The general opinion in Germany is that you may live an unhealthy life of pollution, stress, overeating, drinking and smoking eleven months of the year. But during the twelfth month you take the cure at one of the many spas 'and they will get you into good shape again'. This philosophy has created a proliferation of spas in Germany. Some offer serious therapies and some are well liked because they offer nothing but peace and good air, sunshine and tranquillity. These may be a pseudo-cure but one does not go there for the cure; one goes to relax. Some people have nice, relaxing homes but their doctors tell them that to relax they must get away from familiar surroundings. You must change your 'style of life'.

It is different in Switzerland where the people are frugal and often ascetic. Thrift is a national virtue. The luxurious hotels were originally built for foreigners who were asked to change their money at the nearest bank. The theory is that scenery and natural beauty should not be just admired, they should be paid for. But then I began to meet people, Swiss and foreigners, who went to Bad Ragaz every year and praised it. They said it was an ideal place to recharge one's batteries, to relax, to walk around and play golf, to sleep and do nothing. The kind of place that almost everybody needs once in a while.

Georg Szell, the great conductor, spent a few weeks every summer there. An ardent golfer when he was not thinking of his music, Szell always went to Crans-sur-Sierre to play golf in an Alpine atmosphere but the altitude is almost 5000 feet, and after a few weeks he would step down to the more comfortable altitude of Bad Ragaz, only 1700 feet, and play golf there. Then he would go to Salzburg to conduct at the Festival, and he would go back to America to take up his tough schedule with his beloved Cleveland Orchestra. He once told me that he could not do it without recharging his batteries every summer in Bad Ragaz.

A view of the town of Bad Ragaz, in the North East of Switzerland.

Now that I have been there, though in wintertime when it is much quieter, I understand how Szell felt. There are two luxurious hotels in Bad Ragaz, the Quellenhof, open from April to October, and the older Grand Hotel Hof Ragaz, open all year. Since I prefer hotels that stay open all year I went to the Hof. There is a pleasant continuity of service. There may be the sounds of hammering because in a good hotel they are always fixing or redecorating something. But the hotel, ably managed by Jean Suter and his wife, Germaine, is run on the sensible principle that a hotel should be a temporary home for people who like tranquillity, good service and good food. It is old-fashioned in a modern way. The walls are thick and the place is quiet and the rooms are larger than in the hotels built lately where floor space is at a premium.

The Hof was originally the headquarters of Abbot Johannes II (1361–86). The nearby Monastery of Pfäfers was much older. Monasterii Fabariensis, as it was known in the twelfth century, had two churches and a house for people suffering from leprosy. By that time the Benedictine Abbey of Pfäfers was already five hundred years old, since it is said to have been founded around 740. Around 1240, perhaps two years later, an important discovery was made in the nearby Tamina Gorge: a warm spring, that was said to have miraculous effects for many diseases. This happened during the rule of Emperor Frederik II of Hohenstaufen who decreed, in 1240, that the profession of physicians had to be separated from that of the pharmacists.

Soon after the discovery of the warm spring, primitive tubs were hewn into the rocks of the gorge, and wooden steps were constructed for the patients who would walk down and spend several days in the water. Dr Felix Hemmerli, also known as Malleolus, wrote in his work *De balneis naturalibus hic et alibi constitutis* in 1453,

Like other hot springs on earth the Tamina spring has a value equal to gold. Who wants to use it, must remain six to seven days in the warm water with no interruption except one night when the patient may rest elsewhere. Contrary to other spas, the patient has all his meals in the water. This is done, because to get down to the tubs and to get up again is extremely horrible and dangerous. If the spring would not come out of a gorge but out of a plain, at least 2000 people could bathe there at the same time. The healing power of the spring surpasses all other hot springs in Germany.

Let us talk of its success. The spring heals gout and arthritis. The warm waters soothe the ensnared nerves of the head and strengthen the strength of vision. The water does not make thirst. It heals the itching of skin and flesh. It heals the scars of wounds. Often it strengthens fatigued joints. In short, the spring will help anyone who suffers from pain and anxiety, and hopes for solace. Faith will help a great deal.

An astonishing judgement, that has been confirmed by modern balneological research. Today over two thousand people bathe in Ragaz in private
and public swimming pools, many of them suffering 'from pain and
anxiety'.

During the following decades the fame of the Tamina spring was such
that the celebrated Abbot Russinger, perhaps the most fascinating figure
in the history of the monastery, summoned the famous Dr Theophrastus
Paracelsus von Hohenheim to Pfäfers. It was not a good time in the life
of the immortal physician. He had gone to Sterzing in today's South Tyrol,
and helped to fight the bubonic plague and then came by way of Meran
into the Tamina Valley. A contemporary sketch, dated AD 1600, shows
the Tamina Gorge with a chapel and primitive wooden buildings where
the patients lived and had their baths. The tubs in the rocks were still being
used. Paracelsus must have studied the spring carefully for in 1535 he wrote
his famous balneological study, 'Vom Ursprung und Herkommen des Bads
Pfeffers in der Oberschweiz gelegen . . .' which he dedicated 'to his gracious
Master, Joann Jacob Russinger'.

The book created much excitement, was often reprinted by publishers
who did not care to pay royalties to Paracelsus – no copyright existed –
and made the waters of 'Pfeffers' very famous. He probably spent only a
few months there, but his analysis of the warm spring was exact and was
later confirmed by many spa doctors. In 1629 the lower wooden bathing
house in the gorge burned down; in 1716 Abbot Bonifazius II had a new
house built at the entrance to the gorge, behind the Hof. It still exists. The
warm spring was taken down in wooden pipes. And in 1774 Abbot Boxler
of Uznach had a large building constructed that would house the abbot's
offices; he was also governor of the region. The building is now a part of
the Grand Hotel Hof in Ragaz.

Then came the Napoleonic wars which badly affected Ragaz, at that
time a small village. In 1799 the French Army of General Masséna burned
down the wooden bridge that led across the Tamina Gorge. There was
a strong wind and the entire village was burnt to cinders. It was soon rebuilt
and in 1819 another Abbot, Placidus Pfister, installed pumps at the lower
end of the gorge and set up a public pool for the poor and for beggars.
Finally, one day in 1840, the church bells rang in Bad Ragaz. In front
of the Hof the thermal waters flowed out of wooden pipes. 'It was the beginning of the evolution that made the small village Ragaz a widely known
spa resort', a chronicler wrote. Eighteen years later the railroad from
Zurich to Chur came to Ragaz. A public bathing establishment was set
up in the middle of the village.

In 1868 a Swiss architect named Bernhard Simon was hired to design
the new spa. Simon had for many years worked in Russia and had good

The Grand Hotel Hof Ragaz. In 1840 the thermal waters flowed out of wooden pipes in front of the hotel for the first time.

connections there. For many years Russian aristocrats came to Ragaz which he had turned into an elegant spa with a Kursaal, several hotels and a special zone that was reserved for the visitors of the spa. The luxurious Quellenhof was opened in 1869, and remained one of Switzerland's most famous hotels. Simon died in 1900, but his ideas were kept alive: the golf course was laid out in 1905 in the middle of beautiful Alpine scenery, and was extended twenty years later. The Quellenhof was badly damaged by fire in 1941, and was reopened in 1959.

Today both the Quellenhof and the Grand Hotel Hof have their private thermal swimming pools and modern therapeutic establishments. Unlike in other spas, the cure in Ragaz is extremely pleasant. The thermal spring, which has a pleasant body temperature at the source, is taken down to Ragaz in isolated pipes and loses only one degree. The spring contains few mineral substances; the Pfäfers spring is an akrotherme, more widely known as 'Wildwasser', wild water. It is colourless and odourless, and people going into the hotel pool are advised to stay no longer than ten minutes. Some people who take the cure complain after eight or nine days of lack of appetite, poor sleep, depression and generally not feeling well. After this reaction the patient begins to feel better, more vigorous, stronger. The bathing cure is often completed by a drinking cure. The water of Ragaz seems to have a stimulating effect on many internal organs; sooner or later it will be bottled and sold everywhere.

People who come to Ragaz more or less healthy take a bath before breakfast and then walk back to their rooms. It is much more comfortable than
in the old days, when the poor patients had to walk down the dangerous
wooden steps or were let down in baskets. After the bath you are supposed
to go to bed and rest; if you sleep an hour, so much the better. After breakfast you do whatever you please. Golf players have the time of their life
on the golf-links. The course is said to be one of the best in Europe. For
people who do not play there is a lovely promenade along the Rhine. The
air is very pure and the altitude is just right.

The principality of Liechtenstein is only twenty minutes away by car.
The people of Liechtenstein often come to Bad Ragaz to bathe in one of
the thermal pools, to play golf, listen to the Kurmusik or lose a little money
playing *boule* at the Kursaal-Casino. *Boule* has long been known as roulette's
bad little sister. It looks innocent and inexpensive. There are only nine
red and black numbers (compared to thirty-six numbers in roulette). But
everybody loses except the five when five appears, and the payoff is seven
for one. The odds are $11\frac{1}{9}$ against the player. In roulette, the house advantage is only 1·38 per cent. But the players – cure guests and Liechtensteiners
– still consider *boule* a 'harmless' game.

It is much nicer to drive over to Vaduz, the capital of Liechtenstein,
that strange country between Switzerland and Austria that is only 15·5
miles long and 3·7 miles wide, has no railroad of its own, has airmail stamps
but no airport, offers magnificent scenery from the Rhine valley to the
Alpine grandeur of the Grauspitze (8525 feet), has no unemployment, no
slums, and one of the world's highest standards of living. No one pays more
than twenty-five per cent income tax. One third of the 21,800 inhabitants
are foreigners, there can be no more than one third at any time. The ruling
prince, one of the last constitutional monarchs, comes from a noble family
that can be traced back over eight hundred years. It is almost impossible
to become a Liechtenstein citizen; people from families that have lived
there for generations are still foreigners. Liechtenstein is a famous tax
haven, has no female suffrage (like Kuwait, Yemen and Saudi Arabia),
and the private art gallery of Prince Franz Joseph II is certainly worth the
trip from Ragaz.

Several Rembrandts, a fine Botticelli, Pieter Brueghel the Younger's
'The Census of Bethlehem', a few great Van Dycks and the two early
Rubens masterpieces, 'Portrait of a Girl' and 'The Sons of Rubens'; you
may see them in the Prince's Private Collection on the main street of Vaduz,
along with many other works. At the beginning of the last war, most of
the paintings were in Vienna's Liechtenstein Palais, one of the three palaces
the family still has in Vienna. As the battlefront moved toward Austria,
the paintings were removed to the subterranean salt mines in Lauffen, near

left The awesome Liechtenstein mountains and small lake of Sass. Liechtenstein borders on Switzerland and is very near to Bad Ragaz.

right A corner of old Vaduz, the capital of Liechtenstein.

Bad Ischl, and to depots at Klosterneuburg, near Vienna, where the vaults were high enough for the largest Rubens canvases. Eventually the Prince went to Vienna, had the most valuable paintings loaded on to buses whose seats had been ripped out and somehow the buses arrived in Vaduz at Eastertime, 1945, when the Russians were already in Vienna.

After you have seen the paintings and bought some Liechtenstein postage stamps which are very much in demand everywhere, you may have lunch or dinner at the Hotel Real or at the Park Hotel Sonnenhof. Felix and Emil Real have learned their art in France, they own vineyards in Liechtenstein, make good wines, and their cuisine reflects the principality's location between Switzerland and Austria. At the Hotel Real you may get a *Geschnetzeltes Kalbfleisch* the way they make it in Zurich, a *Wiener Backhuhn*, better than in many places in Vienna, and *piccata toscana*. Also *quenelles de brochet*, *scampi* and oysters, and fine game.

Why am I telling you all this when I should be talking about the cure in Bad Ragaz? Because the closeness of Liechtenstein is one of the best things about the cure in Bad Ragaz.

Meran-Merano

The wide plain between Merano and
Bolzano is full of lush orchards and
vineyards. This is taken from the
Castle Tyrol.

Meran became my favourite retreat one day in 1913 when my mother took me there for 'convalescence'. I was a sickly boy of six who hated food – some people find this hard to believe now – and had gone down with pneumonia and pleurisy. Much has changed since then, everywhere and in Meran, but I still go back there. It is still a place where one can get away from it all for a while. Again, some people will find this hard to believe. It takes some doing since Meran has been discovered by the travel agencies.

During the glittering decline of the Habsburg monarchy Meran was the empire's southernmost spa. Empress Elisabeth, lovely and unhappy, heroine of legends, operettas and Sunday supplements, often spent the winter in Meran, surrounded by her court and the *Hochadel*, the high aristocracy – the ones who would not even talk to the lower, bread-and-butter aristocracy. Also present were Russian dukes, British lords and expensive Bohemian tailors. Also ladies of what was then known as 'easy virtue'. The sort of people who also went to Baden-Baden, Monte Carlo and other fashionable resorts. Meran belonged to that group. The 'cure' was very pleasant. No waters, no baths – that came later – but the spa doctor would advise you to eat several pounds of small grapes a day. They grew in and around Meran, they even have vineyards in the centre of town. The grapes, known as *Kurtrauben*, cure grapes, were not good for the making of wine but if eaten in sufficient quantities they were said to have the effect of the waters of Karlsbad and they tasted much better. Also recommended were slow walks. A former spa doctor named Tappeiner had a beautiful promenade constructed, at his own expense, that slowly ascended the Küchelberg behind the spa, so slowly that it was even recommended to people who had a little heart trouble.

In autumn and winter, when the weather was awful in much of the Habsburg empire, the climate in Meran was wonderful. Sunshine, and deep-blue skies, as on a painting by Paolo Veronese. (Verona is only two hours away.) The air tasted of apples that had been stored in cellars, and it felt like velvet. There were orchards, vineyards, cedars, cypresses, and in the rear were high mountains covered with snow. They almost surround the spa and keep the cold winds away. Unlike most Alpine valleys, which go from west to east, the lower Adige (Etsch) valley extends north-south. Meran is pleasantly secluded. The Brenner railroad and the autoroute between Northern and Southern Europe lead through Bolzano (Bozen) but that is twenty-miles away. In the late spring the wide plain between Bozen and Meran is a vast orchard filled with blossom, with the chimneys of houses sticking out like conning towers in the water. The sight and the scent are incredible.

It could be paradise, but there has been trouble in paradise. After the

Peace Treaty of Saint-Germain in 1919, when Austria had been forced to cede South Tyrol to Italy, the region was named Alto Adige. Meran, the southernmost spa of Austria-Hungary, became the northernmost *stazione climatica* of Italy. The people from Austria went there for warmth and sunshine. The people from Italy who often have too much sunshine and heat, go because there the summer is tolerable and autumn can be heavenly.

No matter where you arrive from – by way of the Brenner Pass from the north, from Venice and Verona to the south, from Sankt Moritz to the west, you will see a fairy-tale landscape, with many old castles and chapels in strange prehistoric settings. Of all the spas mentioned in this book Meran – or Merano, as it is now called by the Italians – probably has the oldest history. Civilization has been traced back to 2000 BC. No other spa in Europe can make such a claim. The Romans loved the region which they considered part of Raetia Secunda. They planted the first grapes there, employing the methods of Pliny the Elder, and built stone towers for their signal fires. From each tower one could see the next. The villages are named after the estates of Roman veterans: Riffian, Sirmian, Schenna, Prissian.

The early Christians also liked the region. Saint Valentin was buried in an old church whose ground walls are near the Romanesque Zenoburg which I can see from my balcony. In 716, Saint Corbinian from Rome came to the region and planted orchards 'cum magno affectu', with much affection, according to an admiring biographer. The first documentary mention of Meran is a deed signed by King Ludwig the Child, dated 875. In 1237 Meran was a market-place. In 1317 it was elevated to a township. By that time medieval knights and rich bishops considered it *chic* to have a castle near Meran. Emperors and popes, warlords and crusaders, came there to relax. Some of them used their castles to invite virtuous ladies. It was said that they could not resist the many temptations – sunshine, wine, the scent of blossom – but that may be hearsay.

The most famous castle was Schloss (Castle) Tyrol, overlooking Meran, which gave the region its name. Dante Alighieri was once a visitor in the eleventh-century castle. A marble slab with an inscription on a Romanesque tower reminds us of the event. (A great admirer of Dante, the American poet Ezra Pound, lived at the nearby Brunnenburg after 1958 for several years.) Margaret Maultasch, the daughter of the Count of Tyrol, lived at the castle. Her ugliness was legendary. (Sir John Tenniel used Margaret, the Pocket Mouth, as his model for the Ugly Duchess when he illustrated *Alice in Wonderland*.) But the Ugly Duchess did not care how ugly she looked, and in the fourteenth century her love affairs scandalized Europe's highest society. In 1363 Margaret handed over the county Tyrol

to the Habsburgs. For a while Meran was the capital of Tyrol. In 1420 Archduke Frederick IV moved his court to Innsbruck in North Tyrol which remains the capital of the Austrian Tyrol. The capital of the region of Alto Adige (officially South Tyrol now does not exist) is Trento (Trient).

When castle life became boring for the shining knights, they would go to Meran which was then a quiet town with four arched gates. Every visitor had to pass through one of them. Three gates still exist and are blocked by tens of thousands of motorists who come there every year during the season. The season is long and gets longer all the time, I regret to report.

The Reformation and Counter-Reformation did not touch Meran and no one was burned at the stake. The Renaissance in Florence, not far away, the Baroque and the Rococo all bypassed Meran. The old buildings are nearly all Gothic. During the Napoleonic Wars, Andreas Hofer from the nearby Passeiertal became the national hero in both Tyrols. He was shot in Mantua and is now considered a martyr.

I have already mentioned the grape cure which, according to a local guidebook, 'is recommended to people suffering from many ills, as well as to healthy persons'. An ideal cure. The old books quote references to the cure by Herodotus, Hippocrates, Pliny, Paracelsus. Personally, I prefer

left The region is dotted with castles, some dating back to Roman times. This one, probably of medieval origin, is the Schloss Castelbel, situated near Merano.

below An old map of Merano showing the town and surrounding castles; even here there are carefully cultivated orchards and vineyards.

Meran.

22. Spital zům H. Geyſt.
23. Schloß Prüneburg.
24. Schloß Thürnſtein.
25. Thürn Gralſchberg.
26. Schloß Gargen.
27. Schloß Labers.
28. Schloß Schena.
29. Schloß Greiffen.
30. Schloß Stamey.
31. Schloß Stabein.
32. Schloß Winckel.
33. Khnielberg.
34. Rundeg.
35. Pflantenſtein.
36. Pfarkirch auff Tyrol.
37. S. Georg in ober maiſt.
38. Anſiz Maur.
39. Prigel.
40. Weingarten.
41. Algunder Pfarr.

the wine cure. The local people do not eat the grapes. Instead they drink the local wine, made from grapes growing on the Küchelberg, and some of the people live to be quite old. Some drink up to a gallon a day. One meets them under the *Lauben*, the old arcades where they emerge from dark *Weinstuben*, as the inns are called. Many wear the traditional vintner's dark-blue apron, even though they have never owned a vineyard. Their faces reflect the colour of the wines of the region, the local Küchelberger, or the Kalterersee, Lagreiner, Santa Maddalena, Sandbichler from other parts of the region. There is also a pleasant white wine, Terlaner, from the nearby town of Terlan-Terlano. These wines are sold all over Austria and Germany, often dishonestly mixed with other liquids. In Meran the wines are clean and honest and they used to be quite inexpensive. Mineral water costs more.

Today Merano is famous in Italy for the Lotteria di Merano, the country's biggest sweepstakes. The races take place in the autumn at Merano's racecourse, one of Europe's most beautiful. By that time the bus tourists have come and gone, and the elderly German matrons and retired

The races at Merano where Italy plays its largest sweepstakes; the racecourse is reputed to be one of the most beautiful in Europe.

professors have disappeared. For a short time small Italian jockeys and assorted Damon Runyon characters take over, plus members of Italy's *dolce vita* set. Eventually, they leave too, and only the local blue-apron wine drinkers remain. That is the best time to see Merano or Meran, when it belongs to the Meraners. The days may be short, but the skies are sometimes very blue in October and early November, the promenades and walks are quiet and the town is again almost as I remember it.

Almost. Merano has changed since the days prior to the First War. There are ugly modern buildings; I never understand why architects from the country of noble palaces build such unattractive structures. There are too many cars, going much too fast. Some of the very nouveaux riches from neighbouring countries have taken over whole districts and live in ghastly apartment houses that advertise swimming pool, sauna and solarium. This is part of progress and cannot be avoided. But the things that really matter have not changed – the lovely gardens and flowers, the rare trees and well kept promenades, forty miles of walking paths. The spa administration employs forty gardeners. In the suburb of Maia Alta (Obermais) one can still walk under vines forming living arcades. Late in August the bunches of dark grapes hang down like red crystal chandeliers. The air oscillates and there is a light-blue haze that gives the hills and palm trees an impressionistic appearance. In such moments one can still have that wonderful out-of-this-world feeling.

Merano's great blessing (some readers may not agree) is the absence of an airport. To take a Jumbo jet you have to go to Milan or Munich, two hundred miles away. There are good trains though and most people drive and see the beautiful countryside. On the plus side, the Lake of Garda, Verona, Sankt Moritz, and the Dolomites are only a short drive away. It is only fifty miles to the Stilfserjoch, Stelvio Pass, over 7300 feet high, where it often snows in August and noted skiers can train even in summer. The border of Switzerland is a short distance away. Two hours later you may be back in Meran, bathing in a warm pool, surrounded by palm trees.

The Dolomites are fascinating, bizarre mountains. A magnificent road connects Bolzano with Dobiacco by way of Cortina d'Ampezzo; it was completed in 1709 as part of the Strada d'Allemagna between northern Europe and Venice. Eighty-seven miles along a marvellous scenic route which stretches past great limestone buttresses that rise abruptly in fantastic shapes. The Monte Cristallo, over ten thousand feet high; the Cime di Lavaredo, a paradise for daring climbers; the Marmolata, highest of all, where you can ski all year round. Val Gardena where some forty ski lifts and cable cars line up the slopes. Ortisei, the town of famous woodcutters. Turquoise lakes, such as Lago di Carezza or Lago di Misurina, reflecting the high mountains. The mountains are famous for their Alpine pink glow

An old photograph of the town of Merano,
situated at the foot of the Dolomites.

that covers the peaks at sunrise and again at sunset. It is a region of legends and fairy tales, of King Laurin and his garden and roses. Two great *minnesingers*, Walther von der Vogelweide and Oswald von Wolkenstein, were born in the region. There is a marble plate on a small farm house in Pieve di Cadove, near Cortina, where Titian (Tiziano) was born in 1477. He often returned to his mountains after he had become one of the greatest painters of all; he lived to be ninety-nine.

And wherever you go in the morning, to see these wonderful sights, you can be back in Merano in the evening. That alone makes it a truly unique spa.

The place has always attracted poets and eccentrics. From the balcony of my hotel apartment I look down at a low yellow house called Pension Fanny. No allusion to Fanny Hill, as some innocents believe. The house once belonged to Fanny Elssler, the famous Viennese prima ballerina who was such a hit in 1840 in Washington and New York. Prior to the First World War, Franz Kafka stayed at the pension for a while, ill and unhappy after a disastrous love affair, trying to get his health back. There is no marble plate on the house.

I remember an old Russian émigré. He had read in a Tsarist guidebook that there had once been a steamship connection between Meran and Venice, and he said he was trying to find 'the secret waterway'. Another man collected stuffed dogs; he had heard that people used to hide money and gold coins in stuffed dogs. Another genuine eccentric, Fritz Herzmanovsky-Orlando, the Austrian novelist, dramatist, artist lived high up in the tower of Castle Rametz. He always carried his movable assets on his person, a handful of gold coins jingling in his trouser pockets. Previous experience had taught him not to trust banks and the gold coins gave him a reassuring sense of independence. He died in 1954, but is posthumously famous as the author of bizarre chronicles and satires of the Habsburg monarchy. His masterpiece, *Der Gaulschreck*, is about a venerable court official who plans to celebrate the twenty-fifth anniversary of the reign of 'His Majesty', most probably Franz I, by presenting him with a tableau containing twenty-five milk teeth. The book describes the court official's improbable efforts to secure the twenty-fifth tooth.

There are cheerful espresso bars where the Italians gather for coffee, laughter and *conversazione*, and Viennese-style coffeehouses where retired 'Old Austrian' civil servants with permanently worried faces read the hometown papers from Innsbruck and Vienna. The clients of the various establishments never mix, never look at one another. A few 'Old Austrian' aristocrats live in genteel poverty in run-down houses, next door to California-style bungalows that belong to wealthy Germans. Tyroleans and Italians have their separate language and culture, and also separate book-stores, delicatessens, restaurants, cinemas, ice-cream parlours and hairdressers. But young people of both groups walk hand in hand, and there are more and more mixed marriages: *omnia vincit amor*.

There has been a great deal of trouble, mostly of a political nature, in the past fifty or sixty years. This is bound to be the case when an old region is handed from one country to another. The German-speaking Tyroleans wanted to separate from Italy and become Austrians, or Germans, or simply autonomous. For a long time the paradise was full of soldiers, bombs exploded, and electric power stations were damaged. But gradually the situation has improved. On both sides there are people who think of Meran-Merano as an experiment in mutual tolerance and international co-existence, a fine mixture of Austrian charm and Italian easygoingness. Perhaps the old Meran was more elegant, but today's Merano is more fun. The old people still have a sense of Austrian *Ordnung*. The new people have imported *totocalcio*, the national soccer pool, noise and laughter.

The mixture seems to work out. The *pasta* and the *trippa* have the same taste as farther south, but here the tablecloth is bound to be spotless. Best

The gardens in front of the Casino with lush plants and tropical palm trees.

of all, the Italians are beginning to discover the region. Italians on vacation do not want to leave Italy. They like to have the pleasures of a foreign country in their own homeland. They go to Aosta where the French influence is strong but one can always have the spaghetti if one does not want the pommes frites. And they go to Merano for Gulasch and Wiener Schnitzel and for the local specialty, *Bauernspeck*, 'pcasants' bacon', home-cured over the smoke of beechwood by the mountain peasants, cut thin (though not so thin as Italian *prosciutto*), the perfect antidote for too much wine.

It was perhaps more than a symbol that the monument of the Empress Elisabeth, that had been banished to a place where no one could see it, is back in the gardens by the Passer, surrounded by flowerbeds. Often there are fresh flowers in her marble hands. No one seems to mind. People on both sides admit that 'this couldn't have happened ten years ago'. Well, it has happened now.

Finally, in 1958, a bath management was set up. Geologists had discovered radio-active hot springs in the ground. Since then the cure in Merano is being compared to the cure in Bad Gastein. Several hotels added installations for the radio-active cure, and other people can get thc various therapies at the Kurmittelhaus (public spa bath house). Experts have found the explanation for the mild climate: it is the springs, of course. Optimists dream of Merano as a health centre, a place for summer and winter sports (there is already a winter resort, called 'Merano 2000', at an altitude of 6000 feet), as a congress centre, and a spa operated throughout the year. The Kurhaus, built in 1912 in lovely Jugendstil, has been redecorated, and is very popular for the concerts of the spa orchestra; and the old Stadttheater, that was for many years used as a cinema, has been restored and is now a real theatre again.

The *International Herald Tribune* arrives in Merano one day late, thus softening the impact of bad news. Television now comes from four countries: Italy, Austria, Switzerland, Germany. Merano remains a paradise, not a perfect one, but I have not found a better one yet. The other day I read what Goethe, who is quoted here as often as the Bible, wrote about the region in his *Italian Journey*: 'Trees and plants subsisting precariously at greater heights here are full of strength and vitality; the sun shines hotly and once again one can believe in God.'

It was quite an admission for Goethe, but he was right.

Lake Balaton

The old Benedictine Abbey was
founded by King András 1 of
Hungary on the Tihany peninsula in
1055. The Abbey has been rebuilt in
the baroque style over the original
Romanesque chapel.

Lake Balaton, two hours away from Budapest, is the largest lake in central Europe, seventy-seven kilometres long and from two to fourteen kilometres wide. Once upon a time Balatonfüred was to the Hungarians what Bad Gastein and Ischl was to the Austrians. To be a Hungarian is a permanent joy and there were widely travelled people who said that Balatonfüred was the most beautiful spa of all. 'Füred' is the Hungarian word for spa.

Balatonfüred truly had everything, beautiful parks, lovely footpaths under old trees, an excellent climate and thermal waters rich in minerals. Doctors in Hungary and even in Austria sent people there who suffered from heart troubles. There was a great spa sanatorium, rather a luxury hotel, where all kinds of treatment were given. But the great attraction of Lake Balaton remains its spirit. Balatonfüred has been called 'a treat as well as a treatment'. The sanatorium – it is now a State Hospital – is world-famous, and has a fine list of celebrities to prove it. Rabindranath Tagore took treatment and felt so well afterwards that he planted a tree there. A few years later, the Prince of Wales – before he became Edward VIII and Duke of Windsor – discovered Hungary, and the British discovered Budapest and the beauty of Lake Balaton. Young men in Hungary began to dress like the Prince, sporting the plaids he liked. The Prince had a weakness for a famous Gypsy primás, Jenö Pertis, and when he and his friends went to Lake Balaton, Pertis and his orchestra naturally went there too.

For the Hungarians, the beautiful lake is a combination of the Lido, of Lake Geneva, and the Mediterranean: a continuous summer resort where people are certain to enjoy two thousand hours of sunshine during the year, where pollution does not exist, where fishing is a great passion, and all sorts of sports are practised. There is excellent swimming, the national sport in Hungary, and yachting with international regattas. For less sportive types there are dances and five-o'clock-teas, Gypsy orchestras, lovely pastry shops. Balatonfüred is proud of its history, its eleventh-century monastery crypt. Not far away is Székesfehérvár, during the Roman Empire better known as Alba Regia, and excavations have revealed ruins from the days of Hadrian. Also nearby is the Tihany peninsula, with a national park, lavender fields and rare birds. Somewhere I read that over eight hundred different kinds of butterflies have been counted. Above the peninsula is an old Benedictine Abbey with cottages that still have the old thatched roofs. The yellow baroque abbey church was built over a still existing Romanesque chapel built around 1055. The church is full of gilded carvings, as befits the Baroque, but the lower crypt is sober and simple with stone columns and with the tomb of King András I. He belonged to the Arpád dynasty. They came to the country then known as Pannonia

in the ninth century and liked it there, no wonder. Even then the region
was a blessed landscape. They enjoyed the climate and the vines which
the Romans had planted.

Something should be said about the fish of Lake Balaton. The State
fisheries department restocks the lake every year, and now there are perhaps
as many as fifty varieties of fish in the deep blue waters. The finest is *fogas*,
which belongs to the pike-perch variety, and is found only in Lake Balaton,
no matter what they tell you elsewhere. A large *fogas*, cooked in a simple
court bouillon, is a great delicacy. A small specimen, not more than two
pounds, is called *süllö*, a glory of Hungarian cooking. In summer and early
autumn the better restaurants along Lake Balaton feature grilled *süllö*.

Scientists have argued for a long time whether the *fogas* in Lake Balaton
was unique or was related to the salmon family. It has now been proved
that it is found only in Lake Balaton and not related to the French *sandre*
or the German *Zander*. Its flesh is pure white and the fish should be 'layered'.
Its flavour has been compared to that of a young chicken. Its back is grey
with dark stripes and its stomach is silvery. The *fogas* eats only smaller white
meat fishes. During the spawning season in April and May, a *fogas* may
lay some 40,000 eggs but only less than a third will mature. In the early
nineteenth century there was some silly talk of draining Lake Balaton. The
Hungarian writer and patriot István Széchenyi wrote in *Steamshipping on
the Balaton*, 'Even if you execute this plan, it would be a crime to destroy

The lake and Tihany
Peninsula. The lake over
77 kilometres long, is the
largest in central Europe.

the most Hungarian fish, the king of the fresh-water fishes. For this reason alone, Balaton deserves not to be wiped out as a modern Carthage.' It was not wiped out.

The most common fish in the lake is *ponty*, carp, which the Hungarians prepare in many ways, and use in Balaton *halászlé*, a red, paprika-flavoured fish goulash. The fishermen in Tihany or Badacsony cook their 'fisherman's broth' in a *bogrács*, a round-bottomed kettle that has been used in the Danube basin for centuries. The success of genuine *halászlé* is the variety of fish used. Optimists compare it to the Mediterranean *bouillabaisse*, but the famous fish soup of Marseille is made with sea-fish and coloured with saffron, while *halászlé* is made from fresh-water fish and has the deep-red colour that comes from peppers grown near the city of Szeged.

Lake Balaton lies in a gastronomically rich section of the country. Sometimes flowers bloom here in December. The region is also famous for its wines which the local people call 'round', when they are light and pleasant to drink, and 'long', when they have fire and heat the heart. Along the northern coast of the lake some excellent wines are made. Lake Balaton was created by a volcanic depression, and the Roman legions planted vines here in the third century AD, during the reign of the Emperor Probus. The lava in the soil and the strong sun that heats the vines from above and from below give the grapes the characteristic taste that makes the Balaton wines very popular in Hungary. They are white and fruity and come from the Riesling grape. The good wines begin in the district of Csopak, a few miles above Balatonfüred where the soil is red and rich. The finest wine in the region is called Badacsonyi Kéknyelü ('Blue Handled') but it is hard to get, especially the 'long handled', that has a small yield and a fine quality. It is a greenish-white wine with much body and bouquet.

Another good wine is the Szürkebarát, known in France as Pinot Gris, where it is used in the making of champagne. In Hungary, the Badacsony variety has a golden colour and is rich and *dolce*, though not exactly sweet. Very popular is also the Csopaki Rizling (as the Hungarians spell the Riesling) which is served with the mixed grill in one of the many *csárdas* in the region. A *csárda* is a dance; it is also a simple inn where people come to have a glass of wine, to eat and to listen to the genuine gypsy music.

This is a place to listen to old stories and legends. A great poet, Sándor Kisfaludy, lived on the vine-covered slope above the village of Badacsony. His house is now a restaurant; one gets there from a narrow road climbing through the vineyards. One sits there, surrounded by vines and hears the sound of violins below. And in the village, near the railroad station, there is the simple house where the noted Balaton painter, Egry József lived; he died in the 1950s. He started as an impressionist but later painted Lake Balaton as he and only he saw it.

If you should not like Balatonfüred, which is improbable, there is another spa in the region. It is Héviz, celebrated for the thermal springs. The milk-coloured waters are warm even in wintertime, of volcanic origin, said to be very good for all sorts of rheumatic ailments. There is a fine hotel on a nearby hill, the Palatinus. The thermal waters are piped into it, and all curative treatments are available. Again there is a *fin-de-siècle* charm about the architecture; some people from England are reminded of Brighton – if Brighton had so much sunshine. The bathing establishments are built on stilts in the lake. There are people, not only Hungarians, who would happily trade the blue sea for Lake Balaton – its charm, its wine, its food and the irresistible spirit of Hungary. Around Lake Balaton one is rarely reminded that one is in the Hungarian People's Republic.

The exotic thermal springs of Héviz, on the south side of the lake. The bathing houses are built on stilts and stretch far into the lake.

Karlsbad

A group portrait of spa visitors at
Karlsbad, Czechoslovakia, in the 1870s.

Two different kinds of people go to Karlsbad now. Most of them have never been there and simply take the cure in the famous spa of Karlovy Vary, now in Czechoslovakia. The cure is known to be excellent and the people go home feeling better.

But there are a few who were in Karlsbad before – one should say before the World Wars – when it was one of the world's most beautiful, oldest spas. They have a strong sense of nostalgia about it.

According to an old legend Karlsbad is called after Charles IV, Holy Roman Emperor and King of Bohemia, who discovered the hot springs there during a deer hunt in 1347. No one believes the legend any more; the present regime does not like legends anyway, not when they concern an emperor. But it is no legend that Charles IV founded Prague University, my venerable *alma mater*, in 1348, and that he commissioned Peter Parler to build Charles Bridge in Prague, the world's most beautiful stone bridge, where you cross the Vltava (Moldau) between baroque statues of saints. If you have ever been there, you will never forget the sight.

Karlsbad is probably much older than its legend. The hot springs that do wonders for people with 'gastro-intestinal disorders' were known long before Charles IV discovered them. The Karlsbad cure is now said to be the most effective in Europe. The waters are miraculous and modern medical science has created half a dozen 'procedures' that complete the drinking cure. Basically it consists of walking before breakfast and again before dinner, and drinking a few containers, called 'becher', of the water. In the early eighteenth century, the poor patients were ordered to drink up to five hundred 'becher', and to spend several hours in a bath, until 'the sickness would escape through the cracked skin'. No statistics exist of how many people survived. Friedrich Schiller, the great German playwright-poet, who was very sick when he came to Karlsbad in 1791, had to drink 18 cups but he seems to have recovered. He lived for fourteen years after his exhausting trip to Karlsbad.

In my family Karlsbad was known as the miracle cure for people who had lived well but not wisely. After eating all the good things for eleven months one would spend three weeks in Karlsbad, drink the terrible waters, lose weight, and one was in fine shape again for another eleven months of feasting, not fasting.

Originally Karlsbad was not for ordinary people. Emperors, kings and very, very important people, who have always eaten and drunk too much went there, since the days of the Roman emperors. Albrecht von Wallenstein, the great military leader during the Thirty Years' War, went to Karlsbad in 1630 to cure his gout. He arrived with an escort of fifty coaches, each drawn by six horses, and just in case the diet was too strong, they brought along fifteen good oxen, ninety young lambs, sixty-three barrels of white beer, and sixty-three buckets of white wine. He seems to have spent three weeks there and was able to walk again, but four years later he was murdered in nearby Eger. But that is a different story which has nothing to do with Karlsbad.

Peter the Great arrived one day in 1711 and liked the cure so much that he returned the following year. He was given a barrel of Rhine wine for his welcome which created a problem for his doctors, but the Tsar did not listen to them anyway. Instead he loved to visit the workshops of the famous local artisans, and ask for instruction in woodwork; he always wanted to learn how to make things. Six years later, Johann Sebastian Bach arrived with his sovereign, the Duke of Anhalt-Kothen. Apparently there was no one who did not come to Karlsbad. Under 'B' the cure list mentions Bach, Beethoven, Marshall Blücher, Brahms and Bülow, and those are only the most important ones.

above Prince Metternich, the powerful Austrian chancellor, visited Karlsbad in 1819, not for the waters, but to conduct highly confidential meetings.

below Goethe, the greatest of German writers, painted by May in 1779. He spent thirteen summers in Karlsbad and was the spa's most famous patient.

Prince Metternich came here in 1819, four years after the Congress of Vienna, when he was very powerful. One knows where he lived – at the White Lion – but he did not drink the waters. He and his assistant Friedrich von Gentz conducted a series of top-secret meetings. 'Even *Cottas's Allgemeine Zeitung* was not permitted to report on it.' The notorious Karlsbad decrees later drastically increased censorship of periodicals, pamphlets, leaflets; placed the universities under the control of government employees, eliminating academic freedom; established the 'priority of positive sciences' over 'philosophical and critical sciences'. Many Karlsbad chronicles fail to mention Metternich's visit; they know why.

Another visit of importance was that of King Wilhelm of Prussia, who later became the German emperor. In 1863 he was not yet emperor, instead he signed his name incognito 'Count von Zollern'. He was accompanied by Bismarck. They returned the following year and met Emperor Franz Joseph 1 but their meeting was not successful: two years later the Prussians were at war against the Austrians and defeated them at Königgrätz. Again, there are few mentions of the fateful meetings in the history-conscious chronicles.

For centuries Karlsbad was known as the *Adelsbad*, aristocratic spa, but after Goethe had been there a few times, Karlsbad became a place for the V.I.P.s of Europe. Goethe spent thirteen summers in Karlsbad, almost two years of his life. He remains the spa's most famous *Kurgast* (patient). The hallowed places where he stayed were The Green Parrot in 1795 (now known as House Madrid) and the Three Moors where he stayed six times, now House Dagmar. The first time he came to visit Frau von Stein, then he became involved with the cure, and the last time he stayed in 1823 at the House Strauss as guest of Frau von Levetzow whose daughter Ulrike was the poet's last love. He was in his seventies and she was only seventeen.

There was no happy end, there was no end at all, only a beginning.

In between he drank the waters and wrote a lot of poetry. He expressed his enthusiasm for Karlsbad in a well known poem,

> *Was ich dort gelebt, genossen,*
> *Was mir alldorther entsprossen,*
> *Welche Freude, welche Kenntnis,*
> *Wär' ein allzulang Geständnis!*
> *Mög' es jeden so erfreuen,*
> *Die Erfahrenen, die Neuen!*

There are Karlsbad addicts who are not happy about the poem because the cryptic confession seems autobiographical rather than balneological.

> What I indulged in, what I enjoyed
> What I conceived there
> What joy, What knowledge
> But it would be too long a confession
> I hope all will enjoy it that way,
> Those with experience and the new ones!

One is reminded of a chronicler who wrote in 1750 about the aristocratic visitor 'who came to Karlsbad to conquer the hearts of the local ladies'. Until 1811 Goethe never brought his wife because she might not be elegant enough for the spa. To Wilhelm von Humboldt he wrote, 'Weimar, Karlsbad and Rome are the only places, where I would like to live.' But he wrote beautiful things while in Karlsbad and in a happy moment he said,

> *Beim Baden sei die erste Pflicht,*
> *Dass man sich nicht den Kopf zerbricht,*
> *Und dass man höchstens nur studiere,*
> *Wie man das lustigste Leben führe!*

Freely translated, 'When you bathe your duty is not to worry, but to think of how to have a wonderful time.' A great many modern physicians agree with Goethe on that.

The poet and super-diplomat from Weimar was skilled in avoiding people he did not *want* to meet. When he came to Karlsbad in 1819, he timed his arrival to avoid Metternich who had left three days earlier. But Goethe publicly regretted having missed the powerful Metternich, 'den gnädigen Herrn', the gracious gentleman. Years earlier Goethe very much wanted to meet Beethoven but the meeting did not work out. Beethoven had forgotten his passport in Teplitz and for a while was detained by the police in Karlsbad. Beethoven appeased everybody by giving a charity concert with the Italian violinist Johann Baptist Polledro, on 6 August 1812. The programme (which exists) mentions 'A great *Fantaisie*, performed by

Herr von Beethofen'. Beethoven returned to Karlsbad on September 8, and at last met Goethe. But the only meeting of the two geniuses had no Titanic undertones. Goethe later noted in his diary, 'Beethoven's arrival. Noon-meal for us. Beethoven. In the evening at the Prague Street.' Musicologists and professors of literature may find a significant meaning in these cryptic remarks. I find none.

After Beethoven and Goethe had been there, Karlsbad became *the* place for writers, musicians, artists who seem to be bothered by the afflictions Karlsbad is famous for. Among the writers are Josef von Eichendorff, Adalbert Stifter, Theodor Fontane, Gerhart Hauptmann, Turgenev, Gogol and Tolstoy. Among the musicians: Schumann, Paganini, Wagner, Max Reger, Richard Strauss and Hans Pfitzner. Brahms came in 1896, suffering from cancer of the liver, and stayed at the House Brussels, but the cure did not help him, and he died in Vienna seven months later. Chopin came as a young man accompanying his parents. Dvořák came five times, never as a patient, but to supervize performances of his works. His music is as popular as ever in Karlsbad. Franz Liszt came as a patient in 1853 and stayed at the White Lion with a friend, Caroline Duchess of Sayn-Wittgenstein. Even the musicians were not aware that Mozart's son was buried at the Andreas Cemetery.

On the tombstone he is called 'The son of the great Mozart resembling his father in stature and mind', but Franz Grillparzer, the Austrian poet, did not agree. 'It was the father's name that destroyed the germ of your energy', he wrote in 1844.

The spa's Belle Epoque was the second half of the nineteenth century when kings, princes and Karl Marx, 'thinker and revolutionary', came there in 1874, and again in the following two years. He stayed at the Hotel Germania which later became the Olympic-Palace Hotel. The police kept him under observation but reported that Marx 'kept to himself, rarely spoke to other guests and often made long excursions by himself'. In 1960 a Marx Museum was opened in the spa. A rather recent guidebook is critical of the atmosphere at the time of Marx.

There were barriers around the springs to prevent pushing and shoving, and the patients would line up for their turn, often waiting a long time. Well-to-do people would hire a commissionaire who queued up for them, filling their glasses. The policemen on duty were strict about the no-smoking rule. The spa doctors had their posts at the Colonnade near the springs, where they stood surrounded by their patients. They wore dignified black coats, and enviously controlled whether another colleague had more and wealthier patients. Competition was strong.

Today there is no competition between the doctors in their white coats who now would not walk to the springs. They are paid a salary by the state, remain in their white offices and see about fifty-five patients a day, which is 'the norm'. On old photographs one sees attractive girls in white starched dresses and white bonnets who filled the cups for the cure guests. The most famous spring was the *Sprudel* (now known as *vřídlo*) shooting a geyser forty feet high into the air, 2000 litres of hot water (73 degrees Centigrade) that contained seventeen different minerals. Of the spa's one hundred and thirty odd hot springs about sixteen are now used, most for drinking, the rest for bathing and bottling; the others are diverted into the river Teplá (Tepl). The word means 'warm'. The springs are structurally different, some have lower temperatures than the *Sprudel*.

During the Nazi occupation, the Germans tore down the beautiful art nouveau style iron-and-glass pavilion above the *Sprudel* because they needed the metal. Now an austere new pavilion has been built, obviously a Russian-inspired glass, steel, and marble structure. The patients fill their glasses themselves, though I saw a Red Army Marshal send his aide-de-camp to queue up for him. The spa doctors were not very esteemed by members of their own guild in the old days. Today the spa doctors of Karlovy Vary are excellent practitioners who treat their patients with great care. Patients are warned not to experiment with the waters or drink more than prescribed, as some would otherwise accept the theory the-more-the-better, since it is all free.

The most famous hot spring, the *Sprudel*, now known as *vřídlo*, which shoots a geyser forty feet into the air. This shows the beautiful iron and glass pavilion over the *Sprudel*, which was torn down during the Nazi occupation.

The drinking cure remains the great leveller. Some treatments are taken in special bathhouses – the political prominence goes to the Bristol, near the Russian Church, where they are separated from the *misera plebs* – but everybody must walk to the springs, walking up and down in silence, sipping the water; loud talk and smoking are still forbidden. The springs are no longer called after members of the Imperial Court but after the Czech princess Libuše, heroine of a Smetana opera; after Rusalka, heroine of a Dvořák opera; after Prince Wenceslaus (they do not like the notion of Wenceslaus being a saint); and there is a Freedom Spring and a Peace Spring, naturally. But the repertory of the spa orchestra has not changed, ranging from Bizet's 'L'Arlésienne' to Johann Strauss waltzes and Dvořák's 'Slavonic Dances'. Attendance is said to fall off conspicuously when they play all-Russian programmes.

Trying to guess the other people's nationality is a favourite game during the sipping-and-walking period in front of the Colonnade. People from the Eastern countries usually wear lower-quality clothes and shoes, but some have relatives and friends in the West, exchange Western currency at the bank for Tuzex (pronounced 'two-sex') coupons and are able to buy Western goods at the hard currency stores. Others buy Tuzex coupons (*bons*) on the black market for Czechoslovak crowns. The fluctuating rate of the *bons* is a permanent topic of conversation. At one time, when I was in Karlsbad in 1970, an American dollar was worth seven coupons. The Tuzex stores often sell good-quality things for less money to the lucky people who have coupons, while the others must pay more money for low-quality goods in ordinary local stores. The system clearly divides the population into haves and have-nots. Prices of some goods are quoted in Tuzex *bons* rather than in crowns. Some people have the notion that the best things in life are at Tuzex. A Czech woman complained bitterly that she was punished for having no relatives in the West. And it was no secret that the Tuzex salesgirls were often polite to Western customers and rather arrogant to their own fellow citizens.

After a while the visitor from the West notices certain things. Many women from the Eastern countries carry large handbags. There may be a sudden sale and they are therefore prepared to queue up and carry the purchase away in the bag. Often a woman's hair-do is more conspicuous than her clothes. Women with blue-grey hair are usually Americans, Russian women love curls, Czech women prefer platinum-blond hair in the Jean Harlow style.

Once in a while, there may be a sudden flashback into the past. Two fragile old ladies with parasols, sitting somewhat lost between the healthy-looking comrades in front of the Colonnade, as though they had been placed there some fifty years ago, and forgotten. An old gentleman with

Kaiser Franz Joseph whiskers accompanied by a woman wearing a Garbo hat. I spoke to him later. He had once been a rich Czech landowner, and he was 'lucky', he said, the regime had kept him as manager on one of his former estates, and now they had sent them to the spa for a free treatment.

After a few days, I noticed cracks in the balneatory co-existence. Many East Germans seemed to ignore the West Germans as they stood in line for their cup of warm water. The West Germans could easily be recognized by their loud voices, and often their women wore gold bracelets. The West Germans seemed somewhat guilty on seeing the East Germans in their cheap nylon shirts. The Czechs, who were the majority anyway, ignored the Russians, and the Russians ignored the Chinese. The Chinese ignored everybody. A few Arabs took no notice of the Jews who retaliated in kind. Only the East Germans and the Czechs and Slovaks carried the Party badge on their lapels. A Viennese couple fraternizing with the comrades turned out to be members of Austria's very small Communist Party. Even some Hungarians from Budapest ignored the Hungarians from New York, possibly indicating a split in the worldwide Hungarian secret society. At the Colonnade, some Westerners felt lonely and lost, and they would furtively nod to other Westerners.

In my 1913 Baedeker of Austria-Hungary, which is worth its weight in gold, the 'Old Meadow' on the left bank of the river Teplá is called 'the always crowded promenade . . . there is an evening corso from 9 to 10 p.m. The tree-shaded Old Meadow ends at Goethe Square and the Pupp complex.' Prior to the First World War Europe's most elegant stores had branch offices at the Old Meadow where you could get anything available in London's Old Bond Street, the Rue de la Paix in Paris, and Vienna's Kaerntnerstrasse. (Today the only good stores left offer the famous Karlsbad porcelain, and Moser-Glass, but the finest specimens must be paid for in Western hard currency.)

The Grand Hotel Pupp, originally built in 1760 by Johann Georg Pupp, was one of the world's great hotel palaces. It was often crowded with English aristocrats, Hungarian landowners accompanied by attractive ladies who were perhaps not their wives, by financiers and plain millionaires trying to relax after eating too much *foie gras naturel*. The very name of Pupp may bring tears to the eyes of a British duke now showing his ancestral manor to American and German tourists twice a week. Around the turn of the century the Pupp 'complex', as it was called, consisted of the Grand Hotel and several other houses, private gardens, and it had its own orchestra. The Pupps also commissioned the noted firm of Fellner &

An early twentieth-century photograph of the palatial façade of the Grand Hotel Pupp, built in 1760 by Johann Georg Pupp, and one of the world's greatest hotels.

Helmer in Vienna to build a neo-baroque concert hall with a large organ. Fellner & Helmer specialized in concert halls and theatres and built many of them in various cities of the former Habsburg monarchy. The first thing any city of 30,000 inhabitants would do was to commission a theatre; it was a status symbol. In Karlsbad the firm also built the Kaiserbad, now called Bath Number 1, and it looks just like a small opera house, with elegant stairways, marble and chandeliers.

For some twenty-five years after the last war the Pupp was known as the 'Moskwa', later 'Interhotel Moskwa', but now it is called Pupp again. The name is too valuable, though the Pupp (and everything else in the spa) is of course nationalized. The palatial façade has been left and there is still the Imperial suite, and several Presidential suites, but many beautiful antiques and pieces of period furniture were thrown out and replaced by ugly modern things. A new wing was added which is respectlessly called 'the crematorium' by the local people. The baroque concert hall was boarded up when I was there. The beautiful old trees in the garden had been felled to make space for a parking lot and a mini-golf course. Obviously much has changed since 1913 when Baedeker suggested that one take the first breakfast at Pupp's Café-Salon, 'several times during the weekly garden concert'. Viktor Karell, a contemporary historian of the spa writes, 'The Karlsbad breakfast, served by the *Kaffeemädchen* (coffee girls) with great care, remained unforgettable to every guest.' The breakfast – coffee, rolls, butter, jam, eggs, ham and other good things – was appreciated even by blasé millionaires, because everybody had walked for an hour and sipped the disgusting Glauber's salt waters, and was hungry.

The River Teplá (*tepl* means warm); some of the warm springs are diverted into the river which runs through the centre of the town.

Music too was important, almost part of the cure. The cure orchestra played every morning from 6.30 to 8 a.m. The music tax for families cost 10–34 crowns, which was expensive, when one considers that a horsedrawn coach from the station to the hotel was only 2·50 crowns, and 3·75 crowns if one wanted two horses. The ride to Marienbad, one and a half hours away, by automobile-omnibus was 10 crowns.

Karlsbad was very elegant prior to the First World War. Wilhelm von Humboldt called the spa with some poetic license 'a diamond surrounded by emeralds'. The lovely Mühlbrunnen Colonnade featured a continuous fashion show. Some ladies appeared with enormous trunks. The cure lasted 21 days, it still does, and no elegant woman would want to be seen in the same dress twice. 'There was always such a crowd that people had to stand in line at least for fifteen minutes to have their cup filled', Baedeker noted.

Even between the two wars Karlsbad was again one of the great spas in Europe. The Russian grand dukes and Habsburg archduchesses were absent, but at Pupp there were still a few ex-kings, all respectfully addressed as 'Majesty', and millionaires and maharajas walked under the colonnades,

opposite The old port of Biarritz, once a small fishing village, which became a popular resort in the nineteenth century.

overleaf left The 10,000 foot Dachstein glaciers which are at the head of the lake, Vorderer Gosausee, near Bad Ischl, in the Salzkammergut region of Austria.

overleaf right Emperor Franz Joseph I's summer residence in Bad Ischl, the Kaiservilla, which is situated in the middle of the beautiful Kaiserpark. The palace's façade shows hunting motifs.

sipping the water as though it were properly chilled vintage champagne. There was Le Corbusier who said the lovely old houses of the Old Meadow reminded him of 'a set of *Torten* (cakes), all in the same style and the same elegance.' There was the beautiful Maria Magdalena parish church, built 1732–36 by the great Kilian Ignaz Dientzenhofer whose masterpiece, St Nikolaus in Prague's Malá Strana, is perhaps the most astonishing baroque church of all, more exciting even than Fischer von Erlach's Charles Church in Vienna.

I was a hungry teenager when I spent a week at Pupp's as the guest of my Uncle Leo, a loyal cure guest of long standing, and what fascinated me most was the enormous Wiener Schnitzel they served at the hotel restaurant. I can still see it in my dreams, and only then, because I would not be permitted to eat such a Schnitzel now. It was so large that its well-breaded sides hung down over the large, gold-rimmed plate like the silk eiderdown over the luxurious bed in my room at Pupp's. It was gold-brown, the colour of a fine Brueghel, the crust had risen without cracking, and the meat was juicy and soft as butter. Uncle Leo immediately ordered a Wiener Schnitzel for himself, though the waiter advised him this was forbidden for a cure guest. Uncle Leo had his Schnitzel and the waiter reported him to the doctor. Uncle Leo confessed his sin. The next day he first bribed the waiter and then ordered a veal goulash, which was also forbidden. The waiter did not report Uncle Leo to the doctor. He would have made a good double agent.

During the few good years of Masaryk's Czechoslovakia I went back to Karlsbad. The spa was crowded with financiers, businessmen, French aristocrats and rich Americans, all of whom had a weakness for the good things in life. And when they came to Karlsbad, they gave up all panto-phagist tendencies and became humble cure guests. Menus and stock market quotations did not exist for the duration of the cure. Nothing mattered but how much they had weighed in the morning, what the doctor had said, and whether the *Sprudel* was more effective for a certain sickness than the Mühlbrunnen. There was a theatre, there were concerts, and always Karl Bayer's *Oblaten*, paper-thin pastries pressed together with almond and sugar filling, that were permitted between sips of water.

And eventually came the glorious day when you had lost five kilos, and felt clean and empty like a well-scrubbed bathtub. You had paid your bills and said goodbye to your doctor. Before going home you would go to Pupp's and order everything a la carte, from *foie gras* to fish to roast duck to dessert, and maybe another dessert. When you got up, you felt like a human being again for the first time in ages, not like a cure guest. You had already gained a precious kilo, but you didn't know it yet. No one stepped on a scale after eating at Pupp's.

opposite The lush gardens in front of the Casino in Merano.

Everything is different today. This is where the sense of nostalgia comes in. Today Karlsbad is a well-run medical business. There is no 'season' (which started in June and ended in October). The spa business goes on the whole year. The aristocratic spa has become the people's spa. Between the *Sprudel* and the Mühlbrunnen one now sees peasant women with headscarves and elderly workers who do not know the meaning of gastronomy and have never lived well. Where did they go at one time when they were sick? They could not have afforded Karlsbad. Now they are sent to the spa by the government, free of charge. People from Czechoslovakia are put up at thirteen state sanatoriums. Guests from other Eastern countries are sent to certain hotels. The Russians stay at the secluded Imperial in splendid isolation. Cure guests from the West are usually sent to the Pupp, the Richmond, the Krivan. They get their visa after paying the price for the 21-day cure. While I am writing this, the price is 1270 German marks (or its equivalent in other hard currencies) and it includes a 'first-class room', three diet meals a day, the entire medical treatment (no more doctor's bills to pay), free transportation of the city buses, and free tickets to cultural events. All you need is a little pocket money for *Oblaten*, and a few hard-currency coins for tips. Officially, tipping is of course abolished, but a Western coin goes a long way in Karlsbad.

The last time I was there I was sent to the Richmond, once known as the Hotel Schönbrunn. It was still a little run-down (it has since been renovated) and some flagstones on the terrace were broken. But the neo-classical façade had been left, and the old park with flower beds. I became fond of the closet door in my room that would open mysteriously as one walked by at a certain angle; one sensed one was in the country where Kafka was born. The bathroom taps were dripping, and there were no rubber rings to stop the dripping but the chambermaids always brought fresh field flowers, and my shirts were more beautifully laundered than at the Waldorf Towers. During the week the central heating was turned on every day, though it was warm outside. On Saturday it suddenly became very cold but there was no heating; the man in charge was off duty. People complained and the heating man retaliated on Monday (when the weather was warm again) by turning on the heating system full blast.

The faulty equipment was balanced by first-rate treatment. The chef was an artist who, contrary to the basic laws of cuisine, produced delicious meals containing almost no fat, no starch, no spices. There were nine dietary menus, for all kinds of sicknesses, and no dish was ever repeated. A dietician nurse would advise you, and teenage waitresses in mini skirts tried to guess your very wishes.

During the three-week cure I had five one-hour interviews with my doctor, a specialist in balneology. After the first, thorough check-up he

An old photograph of the centre of the town showing the Roman Catholic Church; a peasant sells her wares on the edge of the pavement.

handed me a small booklet, 'Prescription Theory', in Czech, Russian, German, English, French, with the diagnosis, my special diet (No. 5), which waters to drink, special baths, mud therapy, hydrotherapy, massages.

'The first week you will be tired', he said. 'The second week you will feel like an old-timer, feeling sorry for the new patients. The third week, you will be impatient and a little depressed.' His prediction was correct.

During the three weeks I learned that the 'Old Meadow' is now called Street of the Heroes of Dukla Pass and the Colonnade, built by Joseph Zítek who had created Prague's National Theatre, is known as Czechoslovak-Soviet Friendship Colonnade, but people still talk of the 'Colonnade'. Goethe, Schiller, Smetana, Dvořák, Beethoven, Adam Mickiewicz have statues in Karlsbad, and the first Soviet astronaut Juri Gagarin. At the former Kaiserbad one is told that Franz Joseph I bathed there, and more

The Mühlbrunnen Colonnade, a beautiful arcade which was the work of Zítek, the Prague architect. It was once the most fashionable promenade in Karlsbad.

recently the Shah of Iran and Juri Gagarin. Metternich, Chopin, Bismarck, Turgenev, Tolstoy, Brahms and Liszt have memorial tablets.

On one of the last days I made a nostalgic pilgrimage to the Hotel Imperial which had always impressed me because it was on a hill overlooking the spa, with two cable car railways going there. When the Imperial was put up in 1912, it was the largest, most modern hotel in central Europe. It was financed by an international company headed by Lord Westbury. Ernest Hebrard, the architect, had no use for the whipped-cream rococo façades of the Ritz epoch, and he did not like Vienna's Secession style. Instead he put up a fortress-like monstrosity with two ugly towers. The cable cars were built by Emil Strupp, a Swiss who also constructed the one going up Vesuvius.

I took the cable car that went up from Lenin Square, near the *Sprudel*. The park around the hotel was more beautiful than I remembered. The flower beds were carefully tended. But the bandstand, once used by the hotel's private orchestra, was falling to pieces, and so was the glass-enclosed garden pavilion where the Imperial's once famous five o'clock tea had been served. Cure guests had been encouraged by their doctors to dance, dancing was said to make you lose weight. The pavilion was now used as a storeroom for broken garden furniture. The paint came off the walls and the windows were broken, yet next to it the tennis courts, which were used, were in fine shape. Such contradictions were no longer surprising. The gravel paths were clean and the hedges were cut but the old wrought-iron lamps above the entrance were broken. It is difficult to replace such lamps.

The lobby seemed darker than I remembered it, and the lights in the corridors were dim. The two elevators that had been used by kings and millionaires were rattling badly. Two new, electronically steered elevators had been installed near the lobby but they were locked, used only by the new V.I.P.s who were given special keys.

There were many rubber trees in the public rooms. In a small salon with dainty lace curtains two Russians in shirt sleeves were playing a game of chess. It was very quiet.

I turned around and went out, to a certain spot from where one had a fine view of Karlovy Vary, once Karlsbad. From up here the spa seemed almost as beautiful as it has always been in my memories.

An aerial view of Karlsbad.

Saratoga Springs and Hot Springs

The pavilion and terrace at Congress
Spring in 1875, showing the 'dipper
boys' behind the bar who dispensed
glasses of the spring waters.

Saratoga is an Indian word meaning 'the place of the medicine waters of the great spirit'. It has been known to the Mohawk Indians for many centuries. They used the spring known as High Rock Spring on account of the huge dome (three and a half feet high, twenty-three feet round) of mineral deposits it has accumulated around it: they believed that Manitou had stirred this water, and freely used it.

No white man visited Saratoga, however, until 1767, when Sir William Johnston was carried to High Rock Spring on a litter, the Indians having assured him that these waters would cure the recurrent discomfort he suffered from an old wound. There is no record of whether or not the treatment worked, but the place was not forgotten: in 1773 one Dirk Schouten cleared a small parcel of land behind the spring and built a log cabin there, only to be forced to leave on account of a disagreement with the Indians. The next year John Arnold of Rhode Island took over Schouten's cabin, improved it, and opened it as a tavern where, for two summers, he entertained visitors, making Saratoga the first pleasure resort in the United States. Among his first visitors were Governor Clinton of New York, George Washington and Alexander Hamilton, who, it is recorded, lost their way while looking for the spring in the forest. Then for a while pleasure was forgotten, the name Saratoga carrying altogether less peaceable connotations. A good business prospect, however, survives a mere battle. In 1789 Gideon Putnam came to Saratoga, leased three hundred acres, and set about turning them into a paying proposition.

Saratoga is situated in the centre of a crescent-shaped valley which extends for seventeen miles from Ballston Spa to Quaker Springs. The mineral waters which, as the place-names indicate, are abundant, issue from a geological fault in the rock. It is three hundred feet above sea level, and surrounded by mountains: the Adirondacks to the north, the Catskills to the south, the Kayderossas to the west, the Berkshires to the south-east, and the Green Mountains of Vermont visible far to the east. The beauty of the situation, the abundant game and fish, together with the valetudinarian attractions of the mineral springs, soon drew large numbers of visitors: any puritan conscience uneasy at the thought of taking a holiday could presumably be quelled by the assurance that the spring water did you good and, moreover, tasted faintly unpleasant. In 1820 a visitor reported that 'the log-cabins were almost full of strangers among whom were several ladies and gentlemen from Albany; and we found it almost impossible to obtain accommodation even for two nights.'

It was soon discovered that High Rock was by no means the only mineral spring in the vicinity. Governor John Taylor Gilman of New Hampshire wandering the forest in search of game, found 'a small jet of sparkling water' at the foot of a waterfall, and on tasting it found it to

Congress Spring, built in the 1830s and rebuilt in the 1870s, was discovered by John Gilman while he was searching the forest for game. Columbian Spring is beneath the small cupola on the right.

be mineral water. He hurried back to the settlement and returned with the entire population – five whites, with a few guests and a scattering of Indians. Everybody tasted the water of the new-found spring and declared it good (the water has a distinctly sulphurous taste). The spring was named Congress Spring in honour of the Continental Congress, of which Gilman had been a member. This has since been Saratoga's most important spring, described in one guidebook as 'her treasure and her pride – her Kohinoor!'

During the next few years a good many other mineral springs were found in the vicinity. These include Columbian Spring, described as 'a tonic spring', whose waters are strongly impregnated with iron; Excelsior Spring, 'remarkable for its crystalline purity, its mineral substances being held in such perfect solution that . . . one must taste the water to receive assurance that the long list of chemicals – sodium, lime, magnesia, iron, etc., are really within its transparency'; Empire Spring; Washington Spring (iron and carbon dioxide); Red Spring (not usually drunk, but 'it has acquired some reputation for beneficial results as an external wash', though nobody could say exactly why); various spouting springs, including the Vichy Spring; White Sulphur Spring, which might be drunk or bathed in; Seltzer Spring; Hathorn, Star, Putnam, Saratoga A, Magnetic, and a number of other springs of less importance. Saratoga Springs could now boast that it possessed the only naturally carbonated water found west of the Rocky Mountains. This water proved very popular: it was bottled and sold up and down the United States.

Various medicinal effects were – and by some still are – attributed to the different springs. The waters are said to relieve gastro-intestinal complaints, gout, rheumatism, anaemia and obesity (though they are also supposed to whet the appetite). They are also good for neurasthenia, wind, certain skin diseases, and the elimination of poisons from the body. The waters are of four types: cathartic, tonic, alterative and diuretic. The cathartic springs contain bicarbonates of magnesia and soda, and sodium chloride; the tonic springs, iron bicarbonate; the alterative, sodium iodide, potassium chloride and sodium; the diuretic, bicarbonates of lithia and hydrogen protoxide.

It is not, given this list of ingredients, surprising to learn that 'the taste of the waters is not always lovely.' However, we are assured that

after the first blush, the water becomes exceedingly enjoyable, and one is tempted to indulge too freely in the pungent, acidulous and salty mixture. The after-effects resemble those of soda-water, and, if a large quantity is taken, there follows a sense of fullness, perhaps a slight giddiness, in the head, and a desire for sleep . . . The iron waters have a slightly inky flavour, and some others leave a sweet taste in the mouth.

The same author warns us that 'In cooking, the spring-waters are worse than useless, unless made into that great American insanity known as "hot cakes". None but the stupid ever eat them.'

By the mid-nineteenth century, various medical persons had set up establishments to take full advantage of the springs. At the 'Remedial Institute' run by the Drs Strong, for example, there were offered, in addition to 'ordinary remedial agents available in general practice', various types of bath, including Turkish, Russian, Roman and Electro-thermal; two types of electricity, Galvanic and Faradic; compressed and rarified air; vacuum treatment, Medicated Oxygen, and a variety of other treatments. In such varied company it is not surprising to note that Mineral Waters brings up the rear of the list of medication on offer (not least, one suspects, because the waters were available, gratis and in unlimited quantities, at all the springs).

That was the respectable side of Saratoga. But, as the century wore on, the spirit of aggressive free enterprise, rampant all over America, penetrated even this remote and somewhat unlikely spot. Saratoga had two assets – its mineral waters and its reputation as a pleasure resort. There was money to be made out of both of them. The opportunity was not neglected.

The Drs Strong might scorn the mineral waters except as a basis upon which to construct the towering edifice of their Remedial Institute; but others were more interested in them for their own sake. There was money to be found in the waters, though it might manifest itself in slightly unexpected ways. Bottling began, as we have seen, early on; but later, in about 1890, a process for extracting the carbon dioxide from the naturally carbonated waters was perfected, and the owners of most of the springs

The pavilion at Hathorn Spring in 1906.

found it more profitable to extract the gas and sell it to soda water manufacturers than to bottle the natural waters whose peculiar taste might not appeal to so many. And those whose land did not possess a spring did not let this misfortune dog them longer than was strictly unavoidable. Obviously, large quantities of mineral water were available – it was simply a question of finding and tapping it. If one drilled a well, who knew but that it might not yield the lucrative bubbles? Accordingly, more and more wells were drilled, with varying success, and pumps installed, until the annual output of mineral water topped 150 million gallons.

If the waters were a potentially realizable asset, so too were the crowds who came to drink them – or who at any rate used the imbibing of the odd cupful every so often as a respectable excuse for the pursuit of pleasure. There were indeed those who patronized such establishments as that of the Drs Strong; and many more who indulged in healthful activities up to a point. 'For best laxative action, drink a pint of Hathorn water before breakfast while walking slowly', advised a guidebook; and, of another spring, 'Take as laxative half an hour before breakfast, then a short, brisk, walk, then breakfast' – advice both excellent and (doubtless) effective, and not too time-consuming.

So far, so staid; but respectability was never – at least after 1863 – Saratoga's chief characteristic. For in 1863 came the races. The Saratoga Springs racetrack is the oldest in the United States, and is as popular and

'Sulkies' rip past at 30 m.p.h. in the harness racing at Saratoga Springs racetrack, the oldest in the United States.

fashionable today as it was when it was first established, largely through the activities of John Morrissey, champion prizefighter, Congressman, state senator, and gambler. The first race there was won by the famous Kentucky, owned by Leonard Jerome, father of the lovely and ambitious Jerome sisters and destined to become Winston Churchill's grandfather. Jerome was clever and witty, and his future family connections were doubtless spectacular; but correctness was never one of his attributes, any more than it was one of Morrissey's. Racing attracts the raffish rather than the correct; and for the next fifty years the Saratoga tone – or a large component of it – was distinctly raffish. Respectable society may be defined by whom it excludes; and the racing crowd was distinctly inclusive. It was a characteristic remarked by a contemporary commentator:

'There are waters at Saratoga presumed to have some inborn curative merits, and in the early part of the season, that is, in the months of June and July, many estimable families betake themselves to the place . . . But in the month of August . . . comes another set of people. A small number of them discover that the waters are there, and perhaps take an occasional sip of them, but . . . they are ignorant of the reputation of the town as a resort for invalids; they know little of the reason for the existence of Saratoga except that it gives territory for much joyous commingling and permits some liberties which are not permissible elsewhere in the land.' It was the 'commingling' which particularly struck the commentator – and not without reason. In the land of liberty and democracy, social stratifications were observed with the rigidity of new religion. The rich had, and remained in, their own enclaves; and there were enclaves within the enclaves. But in Saratoga, 'more than upon any other racecourse, you see curious intimacies existing between many-times millionaires of the "Street" and touts who know not where they may sleep that night. The bugle blows at Saratoga at 2.15. The procession from town begins about 1.15 . . . The main avenue of the town is thick with vehicles . . . Drivers are shouting "This way for the track!" and there is a din and a stir that recalls a New York ferry-landing . . . You may notice in the same equipage a Congressman and a Senator, friends for the first time in their lives. A lady who frequently assists the wife of the President in receptions passes you, tooling her own trap, filled with a party . . . all of whose names are in the Blue Book of Gotham; and following them is a rig, no less stylish, driven by a woman to whom no-one bows . . . Imagine such a procession in town!'

Unimaginable; and, as if the racing did not attract enough undesirable types – as if it did not put enough temptation and bad company in the way of weak-willed husbands and sons – there was, as well, the Casino. This, a fine red-brick building plumb in the middle of town, in Congress Park, right opposite the main spring, was built in 1867, at the instigation of John Morrissey. It prospered – it flourished; by 1894, when it was taken over and further embellished by Richard A. Canfield, 'Prince of Gamblers', it had the reputation of being the most profitable and the most famous gambling establishment in the world, while Saratoga was known as the gambling capital of America. Not that gambling was legal; but nothing indictable went on in the downstairs rooms, and as for the upstairs rooms – well, nobody inquired too closely; income, whatever its source, is undeniably income.

So, when the new century arrived, Saratoga seemed well on the way to perdition. Morals were loose; wine, women and song flourished unchecked; and there was, into the bargain, a very real danger that the mineral springs – the original fountain from which flowed all subsequent prosperity – would soon be exhausted, such were the number of new boreholes sunk, such the abandon with which gas was extracted to put cheap fizz into the nation's soda bottles. The whole thing was a blot on the escutcheon of the sober and correct puritan east coast. The forces of moral and business opprobrium began to mount.

It was the moral – or immoral – front which gave way first. The racing was retained – it was altogether too popular, successful and profitable to be abandoned – but in 1904 the Casino was closed, the official eye having suddenly opened. Canfield, bowing to the inevitable, reluctantly sold his holdings to the city and respectability, in the shape of the Historical Society of Saratoga Springs, founded in 1883 but until this time without a permanent home, was quickly moved in.

Business enterprise, as might have been expected, held out slightly longer. It was, after all, an integral part of that puritan ethic which had no hesitation whatever in dubbing gambling immoral and therefore illegal. But, reluctant as they might be to disrupt the course of private enterprise, the citizens decided they could no longer stand by and witness the death of the goose. The loss of the golden eggs would not only be a pecuniary shame, but might look bad in the eyes of future generations. In 1910, therefore, New York State began to buy up the mineral springs holdings, and by 1912, had taken over 163 of the springs in the area. Of these, it shut off all but 19; many had never been natural springs, but were the result of the speculators' boreholes. The State also bought up the land around the springs, and converted it into State parks.

Saratoga was now (apart from the races) as unexceptionable as might be; but, in a sense, too late. It was now many years since it had been able to pride itself on being a resort of the ultra-fashionable. These had their own circuit, and Saratoga did not figure in it (although Hot Springs did) save for a few fleeting days during the races. Rather it catered for the almost fashionable – the aspiring well-to-do. For these, and especially for mammas with marriageable daughters, there was little doubt that the main attraction of Saratoga was the other visitors. It became a received setting in which one could see and be seen, meet and be met; and to this end one of the great social activities of nineteenth-century America – Hotel Life – could freely be participated in in an unequalled setting.

Not that it was unfashionable to live in hotels. On the contrary: the Plaza in New York had been a home, at different times, to Goulds, Vanderbilts, Harrimans – none of whom, it was true, began by being fashionable, but whose wealth, in every case, was so gigantic that it and they triumphed regardless. And farther west, it was only in a hotel that the basic amenities of civilized life might often be procured. 'The story goes that some cities in the far West are entirely composed of wooden huts, grouped round an

High Rock Spring Pavilion; High Rock was the first known spring in the area, used by the Indians before the White man reached America.

immense hotel,' wrote Paul Bourget in 1893. Bourget, coming from a
Europe where a family would expect to spend most of the year at home
– or, if very wealthy, between two homes, town and country – was very
struck by the itinerant quality of life in fashionable America. 'We call
Rochester our home, but we have spent ten winters here,' he quoted a
'much admired young woman' as saying to him in New York. 'As the ten
winters spent in New York correspond with ten summers at Newport, as
many autumns at Lenox, and probably several springs in Paris, it may be
imagined how much of a place the real home has in the life of such a family.'
Home, in the European sense, barely existed for such people. It was more
a portable concept, which they carried with them, and imposed upon whatever place they might be staying in. 'The family live in the hotel with their
private drawing-room, which they adorn with pictures and draperies, and
often with their own furniture,' Bourget noted. He felt that hotel life, where
the family could live untrammelled by such impositions of a normal domes-
tic timetable as common mealtimes, suited the peculiar psychology of the
American family: 'One must have sojourned in one of these hotels and
dined with these people to be able to realize how entirely the members
of the families live side by side rather than with one another. The wife
or the daughter is getting up from the table when the father or the husband
comes in to breakfast, lunch or dinner. It is a very commonplace, but very
expressive token of that which is the basis of American family life – every
one for himself and by himself.'

It is unquestionably in Saratoga towards the end of the nineteenth century that the American hotel reached its apotheosis. 'Newport and Inter-
laken, Ems and Long Branch, have their special charms, but nowhere is
so much of a caravansary and general splendour concentrated in so limited
a space,' remarked a commentator in 1882. Gone were the three crowded
log cabins, 'little more than shelters', of sixty years before. Saratoga now
accommodated a seasonal average of 50,000 visitors; and the grand hotels
for which it was famous were the largest and grandest in the world. They
lined the main street, Broadway, in highly-finished splendour equalled only
by the varied toilettes and general turnouts of their inhabitants, who
arrived for the season fully equipped with their possessions packed in those
enormous cabin trunks with vaulted lids which came to be known as 'Sara-
togas'.

The largest of all these huge hotels was the United States Hotel. 'The
United States Hotel contains 1100 rooms, and capacity for 2000 guests,'
marvelled one observer. 'It offers an especial advantage to visitors in the
large number of its cottages and full suites of room having a private entrance, numerous connecting rooms, large closets and bath-rooms
appropriated to each. In these are combined the seclusion and repose of

opposite The Tihany peninsula
on Lake Balaton.

overleaf left The modern
thermal building lies at the
foot of the towering structure
of the central town church in
Karlsbad, Czechoslovakia.

overleaf right One of the hot
springs at Karlsbad.

family life with the ease and luxury of hotel living. The cottage halls and parlour windows open upon large piazzas, which face the beautiful lawn; the whole forming a magnificent interior view ...' What most astonished people was the sheer size and volume of these places: 'They have a bewildering habit here of repeating the wondrous tale. They talk about the miles of carpeting; the thousands upon thousands of doors and windows; the hundreds of miles of telegraph wires; vast acres of marble floors; and tons of eatables stored in the pantries, till one is lost in admirable confusion. It is all true and that is the wonder of it', sighed an amazed contemporary.

Once arrived, what did one do all day? Generally – during the week, at least – families were represented mainly by their female members, fathers and husbands being too busy earning the wherewithal to pay the hotel bills. The men, when they did come, were not much seen at the hotel. They were occupied at the casino, at the races, and in other establishments which they did not bother to mention to their wives. Exceptional would have been the man who did contrive to spend much time with his family. This separation of the lives of men from those of the wives and daughters they worked so hard to support was an often-remarked fact of American life.

For hopeful and ambitious mothers, the life of the mind was more active than that of the body. Edith Wharton pictures one such lady taking her ease in the Grand Union Hotel, which was near the United States on Broadway, and was almost as big and quite as grand:

'The thermometer stood over ninety, and a haze of sun-powdered dust hung in the elms along the street facing the Grand Union Hotel, and over the scant triangular lawns planted with young firs, and protected by a low white rail from the depredations of dogs and children.

Mrs St George ... sat on the wide hotel verandah, a jug of iced lemonade at her elbow and a palmetto fan in one small hand, and looked out between the immensely tall white columns of the portico, which so often reminded cultured travellers of the Parthenon at Athens (Greece). On Sunday afternoons this verandah was crowded with gentlemen in tall hats and frock-coats ... but today the gentlemen were racing, and the rows of chairs were occupied by ladies and young girls listlessly awaiting their return, in a drowsy atmosphere of swayed fans and iced refreshments ...

Mrs St George had always been rather distant in her manner to the big and exuberant Mrs Elmsworth who was seated at this moment near by on the verandah. (Mrs Elmsworth was always "edging up.") Mrs St George was instinctively distrustful of the advances of ladies who had daughters of the age of her own ...

A good many hours of Mrs St George's days were spent in mentally cataloguing and appraising the physical attributes of the young ladies in whose company her

An elegant mansion on Union Avenue in Saratoga Springs, USA.

daughters trailed up and down the verandahs, and waltzed and polka-ed for hours every night in the long bare hotel parlours, so conveniently divided by sliding doors which slipped into the wall and made the two rooms into one. Mrs St George remembered the day when she had been agreeably awestruck by this vista, with its expectant lines of bent-wood chairs against the walls, and its row of windows draped in crimson brocatelle heavily festooned from overhanging gilt cornices. In those days the hotel ball-room had been her idea of a throne-room in a palace; but since her husband had taken her to a ball at the Seventh Regiment Armoury in New York her standards had changed ...'

Meanwhile, the daughters of such as Mrs St George occupied their time more actively. There were varied amusements. One could listen to music,

The Grand Union Hotel. It became fashionable in the late 1880s to stay at hotels. These pictures from an illustrated newspaper give some indication of the lavish life which people once indulged in.

or dance to it; but concerts were not the main attraction, any more than were the waters. No; the attraction of Saratoga, from the point of view of eager young ladies and expectant mammas, was the possibility of making the correct acquaintance. There was a recommended itinerary which the dutiful daughter might follow daily: 'Rise and dress; go down to the spring; drink to the music of the band; walk around the park; bow to gentlemen; chat a little; drink again; breakfast; see who comes in on the train; take a *siesta*; walk in the parlour; bow to gentlemen; have a little small talk with gentlemen; have some gossip with ladies; dress for dinner; take dinner an hour and a half; sit in the grounds and hear the music of the band; ride to the lake; see who comes by the evening train; dress for tea; get tea; dress for the hop; attend the hop; chat a while in the parlours, and listen to a song from some guest; go to bed.' Although the compiler of this time-table went on the remark that 'The sensible girl, the young woman with a mind of her own, laughs a scornful laugh at such folly,' there can be little doubt that this did indeed comprise the daily round for a great many. It was a curious, characteristic, naïve and perhaps endearing admixture of blatancy and gentility, and of absorbing interest to the participants.

The music pavilion in Congress Park, one entertainment for the idle young ladies whose main preoccupation when visiting Saratoga was to make the 'correct acquaintance'.

One of the many stately mansions and villas in Saratoga, built towards the end of the last century.

In short, Saratoga is very much an embodiment of that gilded age whose apogee was the 1890s – the age of robber barons and exclusive society, of Ward McAllister and untrammelled free enterprise. It was the age of the railroads, of the private car and the befringed and gilded parlor car, when the New York Central could advertise its 'Saratoga Limited' with pictures of the luxurious observation car, the padded armchairs, the buffet car with such elegantly tasselled curtains: 'Leave Grand Central every afternoon except Sunday, arriving Saratoga in time for dinner; leave Saratoga after an early breakfast, reach New York in ample time for business.'

Certainly this is the epoch which today's Saratoga is making a determined effort to recapture. The old Casino, now restored, is still occupied by the Historical Society, and the visitor can move back in it to Saratoga's heyday. A gaming-room is preserved intact (though not, alas, used for its original purposes) and various nineteenth-century interiors are reproduced. Across the street, the matching exteriors of elaborate Victorian mansions are being lovingly restored: Saratoga is particularly rich in that ornate style of private house architecture known as 'Hudson River Bracketed'. The little pavilions housing the various springs are also receiving attention: that housing Congress Spring, for example, has gone back to Saratoga's remoter past – the early nineteenth century. A simple and elegant neo-classic construction was replaced by the Victorians with an ornate neo-gothic hall; but this, fallen into dilapidation, has recently been replaced by a replica of the original pavilion.

Meanwhile, the spa flourishes. The 'Spa complex', owned by New York State, is open all the year round. 'A large tub is filled with naturally carbonated water, at body temperature. As you rest your head on a sponge pillow your body is painted with millions of tiny bubbles. Each bubble acts as a tiny massage. After twenty quiet minutes you leave the tub for a massage table where the trained hands of a licensed masseur or masseuse relieve the tensions of our modern day world in approximately twenty minutes. Wrapped in hot sheets you are left to retire in a private bed for relaxation and or sleep.' And – 'During off season the rates for the entire experience can be as low as $5.25'. Which must make this among the best value spas in the world. And if you still feel strong enough after all that, the springs still flow, ranging from slightly salted alkaline (the Orenda) through the Haves Well ('a rather strong one') to Hathorn mk 3 ('a very strong Saline.')

After which, should you have money to burn, there is – of course – still the racing.

For those who blench at the thought of being massaged by millions of tiny bubbles prior to a pummelling by the pitiless hands of a masseur, the answer may be the Hot Springs regime. This traditionally consists of lying in a warm pool while mint juleps are floated out to you by a smiling bartender with endless supplies of mint and bourbon. Certainly there could be no greater contrast than that between Saratoga, the lively, bustling northern spa, with its racing and gambling and sharp eye for business, and the sleepy, southern feel of Hot Springs, Virginia.

The contrast is partly due to climate. Saratoga's, in northern New York, is extreme, with long, severe winters alternating with sweltering summers. Winter comes to Virginia, too, but it is short compared with the long, lotus-eating southern summers.

Hot Springs is situated on the western slopes of the Alleghenies, near the border with West Virginia, just east of the Blue Ridge. As with many other spas, it is not isolated: among the other mineral springs to be found nearby are Sulphur Springs and White Sulphur Springs in West Virginia, and Warm Springs and Healing Springs just down the valley.

It is said that the Warm Springs were first discovered by a young Tidewater Indian on his way to the coast. He had been beating his way through the mountain forests; night was falling; he was exhausted. He could see no suitable stopping-place. Finally, in despair, lost and despondent, he threw himself down beside a spring. When he woke up in the morning he found that he had rolled into the water during the night and was wonderfully refreshed, warmed and revived. He marked the spot, went on his way, and later returned with other members of his tribe.

Whether or not this romantic tale is true, it is certain that the Warm and Hot springs are on an old Indian game trail. The road leaves the Shenandoah valley through Buffalo Gap, and crosses the Cowpasture, Calf Pasture and Bullpasture rivers, which, as their names indicate, were once grazing-grounds for the great herds of buffalo. The Indians used both the Warm and the Hot springs for bathing, and the valley was often visited by the Tidewater tribes, though there does not seem to have been a permanent settlement there.

The first of the two springs to be developed as a resort by white settlers was Warm Springs. The first settlement there was established in 1727. There was a considerable population by 1755, and by 1800 Warm Springs was a well-established resort. From the very beginning it prided itself on its southern exclusivity, as compared with the all-comers eagerness of Saratoga. In the records of the old Warm Springs Hotel, dating from 1820, (writes a long-time resident of Hot Springs), 'will be found the names of most prominent Virginians from 1820 on. Family is important in Virginia, and it is amusing to look over these records with Virginia friends.' One

The impressive 'Homestead' hotel at Hot Springs, which is surrounded by hot springs and pools. The Hot Sulphur Spring is shown here.

of these prominent Virginians was Thomas Jefferson, who visited Warm Springs on a number of occasions. On the last of these, he stayed in the water for two hours, and afterwards wrote to a friend that he was of the opinion that this had so damaged his health that he had never completely recovered from the experience.

If Jefferson did indeed stay in the waters for this length of time, then it must have been quite against the advice of any attendant physician. It seems to have been generally agreed that fifteen minutes was the maximum length of time which could beneficially be spent in the waters (and this is still the generally accepted optimum bath-time).

'Peregrine Prolix', a visitor at Warm Springs in 1835, gives a description of the bathing arrangements at the Warm Springs Hotel: 'The water is five feet deep for the gentlemen and four for the ladies. The two sexes bathe alternately; spaces of two hours being allotted, from 6 a.m to 10 p.m. You may take three baths a day without injury. To bathe comfortably you should have a large cotton morning gown of a cashmere shawl pattern lined with crimson, a fancy Greek cap, Turkish slippers and a pair of loose panta-loons; a garb that will not consume much time in doffing and donning. Stay in the bath fifteen minutes, using very little exercise whilst in the water. As soon as you come out, hurry to your cabin, wrap yourself in a dry night gown, go to bed, cover up warm, go to sleep, get into a fine perspiration, grow cool by degrees, wake up in half an hour, dress and go to dinner with what appetite you have.

'This process, except the dinner, may be repeated twice a day with great profit and pleasure, and on one occasion, breakfast or supper can take the place of dinner. At this comfortable, well-kept and agreeable establish-ment, the charge is eight dollars per week, or one and half per diem; and half price for servants and horses. If you want fire in your room you have it for asking, and, in truth, every effort is used to give comfort and satisfac-tion to the visitors.'

By the time Prolix was commenting in this way on Warm Springs, a certain Dr Goode, a physician, had settled in the valley, and had for the past ten years been busy establishing Hot Springs as a rival spa.

The Hot Springs issue from the ground over a very small area; all, how-ever, are slightly different in temperature and mineral content. It was con-sidered that some of these waters might be beneficial when drunk; but this has never been a wide-spread habit at Hot Springs, since it makes no use of the main asset of these waters, which is that they issue from the ground at temperatures which make them ideal for bathing, needing neither heat-ing nor cooling. Quite apart from the convenience of this, it is considered a great advantage from the point of view of conserving the mineral balance, since this may be changed with a change of temperature (or even by prolonged exposure to the air; just as the fizzing waters of Saratoga lose their bubbles if they are left standing).

Dr Goode's main form of treatment was the 'Spout Bath', the bathhouse for which was erected near the Spout Spring. In this bath, the water ran into the bathhouse through a spout about shoulder high, its considerable force being generated by the ten-foot fall from the spring to the outlet. The bather stood or (if infirm) sat and let the spout play on various parts of the body, the water massage having a most invigorating effect.

Many of Dr Goode's innovations may have been taken from the use of the mineral waters at Aix-les-Bains, whose waters, among European spas, most closely resemble those of Hot Springs, but it seems likely that the Spout Bath had been established before his arrival, since he did not claim the invention for himself. Be that as it may, the reputation of Hot Springs as a spa was founded on the Spout Bath treatment. Certainly it was more *recherché* than anything then available at Warm Springs, where the addition of a separate ladies' bath was then only fairly recent: until well into the 1830s there had been only one bath there (subsequently taken over by the gentlemen) into which one could step, plunge, or be lowered in an invalid chair.

In 1846, Dr Goode opened a 'Modern Hotel' at Hot Springs which he called The Homestead, following a local tradition: the first 'Homestead' had been built there around 1756, although it could hardly have been

The Homestead was first built in 1756, but it has been rebuilt several times since then. This shows the hotel in 1923. Riders are preparing for a trip on the trails, outside the impressive columned entrance.

called 'modern' or even comfortable. Over the next half-century, the bathing facilities at Hot Springs became steadily more varied. The main building was the 'Pleasure Pool', which was in a rectangular building about one hundred feet by a hundred and twenty-five. This was partitioned in the middle to make two pools, one for men, one for women. The tradition was always that the men bathed naked, but the ladies wore a strange bathing-dress one description of which likens it to a pillow-case with holes cut in the corners. The water in the pleasure pool was a mixture from all the springs, the largest, hottest and most strongly-flowing of which was called the Boiler Spring. Then there was the Spout Bath; and the Plunge, which was cooler than the other springs used for treatments, its temperature being only about eighty-six degrees.

Pleasant though all this might be, Hot Springs might have remained a small watering place like any other, had it not been for the coming of the railroads. The fashionable and bustling spa it was to become was a true product of the railway age.

The development of Hot Springs as a spa took place towards the end of the last century. The group which developed it was a syndicate which bought up the Chesapeake and Ohio Railroad. Their plans naturally included the development of the hinterland served by this railroad, since the more development, the more business: a railroad was as rich as its hinterland was prosperous and diverse. Their plans for Virginia included steamship lines and coalfields, and also – one member of the syndicate was particularly enthusiastic about this idea – the idea of restoring the mountains of Virginia in the public mind as a good place for vacations, a role they had once filled but for which they were now less popular. Accordingly, the financiers were ferried around the various Virginia springs to see which seemed most suitable for promotion in such a development. Their first thought was White Sulphur Springs, but that was ruled out when the shoes of a leading member of the party, George T. Bliss, became mildewed during an overnight stay there. Mr Bliss refused to put money into a place subject to river fogs.

As a result of this trip, the syndicate decided to buy the three springs in the Cowpasture Valley: Warm, Hot and Healing Springs. At the same time the railroad undertook to build a branch to the valley from the main line at Covington, Virginia, and for many years this remained the main means of access to the valley. A fine railway hotel was also built in the traditional manner at the terminal, but it was realized too late that it would (naturally) be subject to smuts, steam and noise, and that customers might feel this detracted from the peace and cleanliness which were, after all, the prime attractions of a spa. For this reason it never became as popular as the Homestead, which was at this time enlarged and remodelled.

Having sunk all this cash into the scheme, the syndicate set about promoting their investment. In 1892 a lot of new cottages for 'furriners' were built along the valley; but it was not until the advent of modern plumbing and efficient central heating made Hot Springs a viable spring and autumn, as well as a summer resort, that the place began to acquire the image for which it was to become famous. For if Saratoga could pride itself on the wide mixture of people who came there to amuse themselves, drawn by the racecourse and the casino, Hot Springs prided itself on just the opposite: its exclusiveness.

Hot Springs quickly became the most fashionable spa in the United States. Spearheaded by the promoting financiers and their wives, the rich and modish took it up until spring and autumn at Hot Springs became recognized stops on the yearly merry-go-round of the ultra-fashionable. One spent the winter in New York; moved to Hot Springs to shed the accumulated deposits of terrapin and canvasback duck; spent the late spring in the country, the early summer in Europe, especially Paris, where wives and daughters would stock up on the next year's clothes; then back to Newport or Bar Harbor; to Hot Springs once again in October, to limber up for the coming winter's intake; and so back to New York. At the turn of the century the popularity of the place among the best people was such that Henry Ford, John D. Rockefeller and Andrew Mellon all went regularly to Hot Springs. Businessmen fought proxy battles from their poolside seats; huge concerns changed hands there; new trends took shape in the languid Virginia air; tensions mounted and were efficiently dispersed.

John D. Rockefeller Snr, the oil magnate. He is here seen in the late nineteenth century. He was a regular visitor to Hot Springs.

It was not only the businessmen who needed a period of recovery. If they had a hard time accumulating their millions, their wives underwent equal pressures disbursing them in a suitable manner. Mrs W. K. Vanderbilt (*the* Mrs Vanderbilt of her era) went regularly twice a year to Hot Springs. 'The demand upon her tact, time and energy grew so great that when she finally arrived at Hot Springs for her semi-annual rest, she was close to exhaustion,' wrote her son Cornelius. She echoed the *mot* of Mrs John Drexel: 'This having to keep *en evidence* all year! We society women simply drop in harness!'

Mrs Vanderbilt (an enthusiastic exponent of Hotel Life) stayed at The Homestead, and, once arrived,

'Mother seemed to crave the shelter of anonymity. Here she retreated into a large suite insulated at each end and overhead with empty rooms so as to exclude all possible sound of human voices. She came to dread the stir her arrival caused at the imposing Greek-columned front entrance and slipped in and out of an inconspicuous door at the rear used for unloading guests' baggage. Here her carriage waited to pull her sedately through the quiet forests on her afternoon drives. At the Homestead, Mother gave no parties and attended none, and seldom dined downstairs, preferring instead to eat alone by the fire in her large private dining-room. Her personal waiter, John, had orders to bring her entire meal at once, to remove the silver covers and depart. I remember one day watching her sitting by her hotel window, a pink French blanket across her knees, her brown dog in her lap. The room was filled with high, dark, old-fashioned mahogany furniture which the management kept just for her visits.'

After some five or six weeks of this regime, Mrs Vanderbilt felt strong enough to take up once again her role as the leading society hostess of the day.

Not everyone who visited Hot Springs, at the Homestead or elsewhere, lived in such style – few could afford to. But the Vanderbilts, Rockefellers, Mellons, Fords, had done their work. Hot Springs had acquired the reputa-tion it was henceforth to keep. It was *the* place to go, not because of the waters – though they were very nice, to be sure – but because *the* people went there. Such became its reputation for restoring the powers of tired financiers that during the 1920s a broker's office was opened at The Home-stead, in constant communication with New York: in the morning, every chair in the place would be filled. 'In April and October it seemed as if the New York Stock Exchange would have to close, so many of the brokers and their wives were at Hot Springs,' recalls the then proprietor of the Homestead, adding: 'They were a happy lot, and if not carefree [they had] a great desire to have a good time.' No, they were not carefree, and after 1929 there was a sudden decline in the clientèle. But times picked up, and by the mid-1930s fashionable ladies and gentlemen had returned, to de-plore the New Deal while riding out in perfectly-cut jodhpurs or swinging a golf club.

Like many places whose reputation and clientèle seem assured, Hot Springs evinced no particular desire to keep up with the times – rather the contrary: if people wanted to come there they could take it or leave it as it stood. What had been good enough for Vanderbilts was still good enough fifty years later. For example, the local population put up a deter-mined resistance to the automobile. As late as 1949 the anti-car lobby ensured that many of the roads in the neighbourhood were still passable only by horse, surrey or buckboard. A similar war was waged on gambling: Hot Springs had a very particular reputation to conserve. It was not going to allow its casino to fall into the hands of professional gamblers as had happened at Saratoga – and look how the clientèle of the place had declined after *that*. This war, too, was won, but only at a high price: the gamblers stayed away, but only because they were bought out for a very large sum.

No, those who come to Hot Springs must make do with the most sedate and respectable ways of passing the time. Golf, for example, was introduced purely on account of its effect on the health. A local habitué, a metal working king, had suffered a health breakdown during World War One. He was recommended to a doctor by a friend, and reported his consultation thus: 'I went to see your friend, but thought he was just like the rest of them. I was sure of it when he got up after making his examination and said he was going into the next room to get a pill which would cure me. He said I must take it at least three times a week and, if I would, I would not worry about anything else and would get well. I was disgusted. He came back and handed me two pills about an inch in diameter, and what do you think they were? – golf balls! I was mad but I gave them a chance, and, do you know, they really cured me.' Having thus received the medical seal of approval, a golf course was constructed at Hot Springs.

Hot Springs is still a fashionable resort, although times have changed insofar as access these days tends to be by road rather than rail, despite the best efforts of the old-timers. We may well envy the habitués their julep parties in the warm pool. But will anything ever match the party held in 1898, at the height of the Spanish-American war, and attended by the Chinese Minister in Washington, who crowned the evening by rising, in his yellow-and-gold robes, and declaring: 'I must tell you how much I admire your country. Now I will sing your national anthem in Chinese.' At which he proceeded to render, rather flat, 'There'll be a Hot Time in the Old Town Tonight.'

Regrettably, neither Chinese ambassadors nor spas are what they once were.

A secluded pool at the back of the Homestead Hotel.

Acknowledgments

Photographs were supplied or are reproduced by kind permission of the following (numbers in italics indicate colour pictures):

J. Allan Cash Ltd 60

Austrian National Tourist Office, London 98, 110, 122

Bad Homburg – Kur und Kongress GmbH 73

Baden-Baden – Bäder und Kurverwaltung 49

Bath Reference Library 3, 22–3

Belgian Tourist Office, London *17*

Bildarchiv der Österreichische Nationalbibliothek 103

George Bolster 178, 181, 183, 187, 194

Brighton Borough Council 35

Budapest Tourist Information Service 155

Cooper-Bridgeman Library *38–9*

Czechoslovakian Tourist Office, London 168, 177, *190*

Douglas Dickins 102, 114, 140, 150 *170, 172,* 184, *192,* 196

EPL/David Williamson *189*

Robert Estall *171*

Mary Evans Picture Library Endpapers 50, 54–5, 68–79, 164, 195, 206

Fotomas Index 11, 14–15, 31, 66, 79 80, 92, 112–13, 145

French Government Tourist Office, London 74, 85, 86, 91, 94

Gastein Museum 118–19, 125, 126–7

Gastein Tourist Office 124

Grand Hotel Hof Ragaz 136

Robert Harding Associates 25, *191*

Michael Holford *18*

The Homestead, Hot Springs, USA 199, 201, 205

Angelo Hornak *37,* 62, 63

Hungarian Embassy, London 152, 157

Italian State Tourist Office (ENIT) 146

A. F. Kersting 8, 12, *20, 40,* 43, 44 (above and below), 46, 52, 59, 176

Keystone Press Agency 203

Mansell Collection 1, *19* (above and below), 21 (left and right), 23, 28, 36 (above and below), 53, 71, 78, 90 (above), 158, 161 (above and below), 167, 175

Picturepoint *169*

Radio Times Hulton Picture Library 7, 32, 106–7, 108, 148–9

Roger-Viollet, Paris 90

Stadtamt Bad Ischl 101

Swiss National Tourist Office 130, 133, 138, 139

Victoria and Albert Museum 77, 82–3, 88, 93, 144

Victoria Art Gallery, Bath 26

Weidenfeld and Nicolson Archive 120, 128

Index